Deal with it

Bullying & Conflict Resource Guide

James Lorimer & Company Ltd., Publishers
Toronto

James Lorimer & Company Ltd., Publishers acknowledges the financial support of the Government of Canada through the Canada Book Fund for our publishing activities. We acknowledge the support of the Government of Ontario through the Ontario Media Development Corporation's Ontario Book Initiative.

Illustrators: Geraldine Charette: Cyberbullying; Brooke Kerrigan: Bullying; Remie Geoffroi: Teasing; Steven Murray: Arguing, Fighting, Racism; Ben Shannon: Cliques; Dan Workman: Gossip

FSC
Mixed Sources
Product group from well-managed
forests and other controlled sources
Cert no. SW-COC-002358
www.fsc.org
© 1996 Forest Stewardship Council

James Lorimer & Company Ltd., Publishers
317 Adelaide Street West, Suite 1002
Toronto, Ontario, Canada
M5V 1P9
www.lorimer.ca

Distributed in the United States by:
Orca Book Publishers
PO Box 468
Custer, WA USA
98240-0468

Printed in Canada

Table of Contents

Introduction 5

Arguing:
Deal with it word by word by Yolanda Hogeveen. 8

Bullying:
Deal with it before push comes to shove by Heather Jessop. 17

Cliques:
Deal with it using what you have inside by Harriet Zaidman 26

Cyberbullying:
Deal with it and ctrl alt delete it by Heather Jessop 35

Fighting:
Deal with it without coming to blows by Rachelle Duffus 44

Gossip:
Deal with it before word gets around by Wendy Doucette 53

Racism:
Deal with it before it gets under your skin by Wendy Doucette 62

Teasing:
Deal with it before the joke's on you by Wendy Doucette 71

Contributors 80

Additional Resources 81

Introduction

Every day, in every school, students are faced with conflicts. As an educator, this guide will help you plan lessons that empower students to deal with these conflicts. This hands-on approach to the exploration of everyday issues will encourage students to think critically about these topics and find their own voice so that they can play a key role in creating safer schools and safer communities.

For each topic, the guide offers a number of informative and enjoyable discussion questions and teaching activities that allow for in-depth coverage of the issues of conflict from every angle. This not only encourages students to analyze their own behaviors and reactions to conflict, but to also look at a situation from the viewpoint of others.

Guide Map

This resource guide covers eight topics in the Deal With It series. You will see that the topics are arranged alphabetically. The material for each topic stands alone, and can be used without reference to the others. However, you may want to consider consulting aspects of other topics which deal with common themes.

The **Before You Begin** section on the first page of each topic will provide suggestions to help you consider the specific needs and interests of your class. The material in the Deal With It books and this guide is of value to students ages 9+. Educators should be aware of the needs and interests of the age group of their students. The **Before You Begin** section of each topic will outline any particular scenarios presented in the books that may be sensitive to younger students.

The large number of discussion questions and teaching activities allow for you to choose those that will be most relevant to your students. Activities can also be altered according to the age group and amount of time you have for a unit — some activities can be completed in a matter of minutes, and some provide an extension to follow up on the students' progress on projects over the unit or school year.

Consider the diversity of your class and be aware of sensitive issues. Think of how the students interact and choose questions and activities that will allow each student to be heard.

Think of the interests of your students and how they can be worked into the discovery of these topics. If your students are tech savvy, choose activities that let them present the information they have learned online, or through new media presentations. If they're movie buffs or book lovers, have them bring in materials that relate to the topics, and have them speak about what these materials have helped them to learn. Encourage a network of professionals that can help students look at conflicts from different angles, and encourage fellow educators to discuss lesson plans and utilize activities in the subject areas that they cover.

The organization of this guide corresponds with that of the Deal With It books. Each topic is split into four sections:

- A **101** section, which focuses on introducing students to a topic;
- An **instigator** section, where the focus is on students who instigate issues;
- A **victim** section, which focuses on kids who feel victimized by the issue;
- A **witness** section, with tips for those caught in between.

Each section encourages students to understand their own emotions and actions as well as to understand the emotions and actions of others. Feel free to jump to sections or spend more time on sections that you feel will be of most value to your students.

In each of these four sections, you will find **Highlights, Discussion Questions,** and **Teaching Activities.**

Highlights

The **Highlights** section briefly captures the main points that you will want to review with students.

Discussion Questions

The **Discussion Questions** are designed to introduce students to the topics and encourage them to think critically about the topics at hand. Feel free to pick and choose the discussion questions that you feel will be most valuable to your class.

Teaching Activities

The **Teaching Activities** are arranged by corresponding page number, and designated as activities for Individuals **(I)**, Pairs **(P)** or Groups **(G)**. Subject Area(s) for each activity is also listed in the **Teaching Activities** charts. Beyond allowing for a range of diverse activities, this list of subject areas allow for flexibility in connecting topics across multiple areas of study, which will help students think about these issues in new ways and to find connections in school classrooms and at home. It also encourages students with different interests to explore issues in mediums and contexts that they are interested in and enjoy. Where possible, research activities focus on Canadian examples.

Subject areas covered:

- Arts (visual, music, drama)
- Canada and World Studies
- Guidance and Career Education
- Health and Physical Education
- Language Arts
- Mathematics
- Media Literacy
- Science
- Social Responsibility
- Social Studies

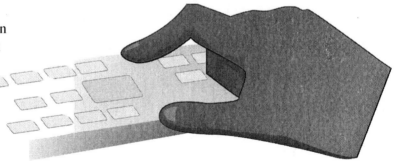

Additional Resources

The guide concludes with a list of **Additional Resources** specific to each topic.

Arguing:
Deal with it word by word

Conflict is inevitable. As children grow up and expand their social circles, they encounter more situations in which disagreements can occur. It is important for students to understand the difference between a disagreement and an argument. Young people need guidance to make the distinction between the two and recognize that arguing is a counterproductive way to deal with disagreements.

    Teaching kids that differences can be resolved in positive ways can be challenging. *Arguing: Deal with it word by word* was created to give young people the tools and strategies they need to successfully meet this challenge. This resource guide uses real-life examples and activities to help show students how to disagree constructively without arguing, while improving their social skills and giving them the power to deal with adverse situations.

Before You Begin
Here are some tips and suggestions to help you plan your arguing unit:
- Gather materials from a variety of sources, including the Guidance Office, social services organizations, articles from magazines and newspapers, and age-appropriate books.
- You may wish to invite a guest speaker to talk to your class. Having an expert on the issue of arguing or conflict resolution will signify to the students that this is a serious topic and that there are professionals out there who can help.
- Create a pre-test or use an on-line survey (such as PollDaddy.com or SurveyMonkey.com) to introduce the topic and vocabulary terms. This activity will also help you and your students to gauge their level of knowledge and experience in dealing with conflict.
- As a class, brainstorm a list of words students associate with arguing. You may need to prompt them to include positive terms such as compromise, resolution, negotiation, etc.). Post this list in the classroom and use it as a reference throughout your unit.
- Be aware that class discussions may be painful for some students as they touch on personal issues in their families. Some students may reveal more about their home life than can be dealt with in a classroom setting. You may want to alert your guidance counsellor or involve him or her in some of your class discussions.
- Students need to be aware of the subtle and more obvious differences between sharing a valid opinion and being argumentative or defiant. Try to guide the Challengers in your classroom by letting them know when it is appropriate to offer an opinion and how to do so in a sensitive and respectful manner. This approach will benefit the student and create an environment for exchanging ideas in a positive, constructive way.

Arguing 101

Highlights

- All people get into disagreements because everyone has their own personal point of view and opinion. You cannot agree with everyone all of the time.
- Disagreements can turn into arguments when:
    - ☛ someone's feelings get hurt or he or she takes it personally
    - ☛ a lot of emotion is involved or you worry about the issue for a long time
    - ☛ they involve misunderstandings, ongoing feuds, or revenge
- Conflict and arguing can lead to stress, heath problems, and violence.
- People deal with arguing in different ways. You might be a Challenger who needs to win every argument, a Dodger who will avoid arguing at all cost, or a Peacemaker who acts like a referee to resolve conflicts.

Discussion Questions

- What are some words you associate with arguing? What do they mean? Why do you connect them to arguing?
- What emotions do you feel when you are in an argument? What could you do to change these feelings so that you do not lose your temper?
- How do you act during an argument? What physical sensations do you have in your body? How might you act differently to prevent an argument?
- How is arguing portrayed in the media, especially television? Why do you think that conflict is such an important part of drama?
- What does an argument look like? What does it sound like? What does it feel like?
- What is the difference between a disagreement and an argument? Explain your thinking.
- How can conflicts be resolved without arguing? What are some things you could do to prevent an argument in the first place?
- Do you think issues get resolved during an argument? Why or why not?
- With whom do you argue the most? What do you argue about?

Teaching Activities

I = Individual   P = Pair   G = Group

Section	Subject Area	Activities
pp. 2–5	Language Arts (I)	After students have brainstormed a list of words they associate with arguing, have them use these words to create a crossword puzzle. (You may wish to have them search the Internet to find and use a crossword-puzzle maker.) Encourage them to look up the definitions of these words to help them write their clues. When they are finished, have them challenge another student to solve their puzzle.
pp. 2–5	Social Studies/ Canada and World Studies (G)	Have students research to find out about a conflict in Canada. Encourage them to discover how and why these conflicts started and how they were or might be resolved. You may wish to have them include information on peacekeepers, negotiators, and treaties. Have students prepare a report and present their findings to the class.
pp. 6–7	The Arts (visual)/ Guidance and Career Education (I)	Ask students to read the comics and think about the four reasons for arguments presented. Encourage them to think of another reason for arguing and to create their own comic to show how the argument might be resolved in a positive way. Finished comics may be displayed in the classroom or compiled into a class book.
pp. 8–9	Language Arts (P/G)	In pairs, have students come up with three more quiz scenarios and possible responses. When they are finished, have pairs switch their questions and answer the new quiz questions. As a class, discuss the responses of the Challenger, the Dodger, and the Peacemaker and the possible outcomes in each situation.
pp. 10–11	Media Literacy/ Guidance and Career Education (I)	Have students create their own "Dear Conflict Counsellor" message or bulletin board. Ask them to write letters from the point of view of a character from a TV show or movie asking for advice about an argument they have had with another character. Have them post their letters on the board and encourage other students to respond, offering suggestions on how the situation could be resolved in a positive way. Review the responses and compare them to how these problems are solved on the TV shows or in the movies. Discuss the differences as a class.
pp. 12–13	Science/Health and Physical Education (I/G)	Ask students to review the "Did You Know?" section. Have them research to find out more about these facts and how people can help prevent health problems by dealing with anger and negative feelings in a positive way. Have students use their findings to create a poster, brochure, or slideshow to give other students tips on how to manage their feelings and avoid health problems.

The Challenger

Highlights

The Challenger is someone who picks arguments or always has to win them once they start. Challengers may have trouble controlling their emotions or feel the need to control other people.

- The Challenger might start or continue an argument by:
    - bulldozing over other people's feelings and opinions by trying to intimidate them
    - bringing up old issues and problems
    - attacking his or her opponent's personality, views, or values
    - dismissing a problem or issue as not worth his or her time or energy
    - blowing an issue or problem out of proportion
- You can help resolve conflicts instead of perpetuating them by trying to:
    - calm down and not take your anger or frustration out on others
    - understand other people's points of view to reach a mutual agreement
    - talk to a trusted adult about why you might be getting into arguments

Discussion Questions

- Why do you think someone might want to challenge everything everyone says?
- Do you know someone who is confrontational or often gets into arguments? How does this make you feel? How do you deal with this person and your feelings?
- Why do you think some people might get into arguments more often than others?
- Do you find yourself getting into lots of arguments? Are there particular people who you argue with more than others? How do you feel during an argument?
- What do you, or people close to you, argue about? How do discussions about these topics turn into arguments? Does arguing ever solve the problem?
- List some situations where voicing an opinion may be desirable and appropriate. What is the difference between having an opinion and being opinionated? How might you express your opinion in such a way that you don't offend anyone?
- What traits might the Challenger share with a good leader? How could these traits be used to help develop leadership skills?

Teaching Activities

I = Individual   P = Pair   G = Group

Section	Subject Area	Activities
pp. 14–15	Science/Guidance and Career Education (I)	Have students research to find out about a scientist who challenged conventional thinking (e.g., Frederick Banting and Charles Best, Wilder Penfield, etc.). Encourage them to find information about the conventional thinking of the times and how this scientist challenged society with their ideas. Have students present their findings to the class, including information on how the scientist found a way to present their ideas so that others would understand and accept them.
pp. 14–15	Language Arts (G)	Have students work in small groups to review the letters and responses. Ask them to choose one of the scenarios and write a letter to the characters involved, giving them suggestions on what they might say to help avoid arguments in the future. Ask groups to present their ideas and discuss them as a class.
pp. 16–17	Language Arts/ Guidance and Career Education (I)	Have students take the quiz and think about their responses. Ask them to write a journal entry about how they feel when they are in an argument and to include strategies for how they might deal with conflict in a more positive way. Encourage students to revisit their strategies and add to them as they learn more throughout the unit.
pp. 18–19	Media Literacy (I/G)	Tell students that they are going to investigate the role of the Challenger in the media. Have them use the descriptions on pp. 18–19 as a guide for the kinds of behaviours they will be looking for. Ask them to create a chart on which they will record the name of the TV program, the character, the role of the character in the program, how they act during confrontations, and whether their actions are portrayed in a positive or negative way. Have students complete the chart over the course of a week. Ask students to share their findings with the class and discuss whether or not characters in the media are good role models for resolving arguments.
pp. 18–19	The Arts (visual) (I/G)	Have students create a poster or slideshow encouraging people to follow the "Do's and Don'ts" on p. 19. Ask them to present their posters or slideshows to the class, encouraging them to explain how they will convince others to avoid arguments.

The Dodger

Highlights
- The Dodger is the person who will do almost anything to avoid arguments or who always backs down and does not express his or her opinion.
- The Dodger might bottle up his or her emotions or need support to express them.
- Instead of fighting back or giving up, you can learn to resolve disagreements and avoid confrontations by:
  - ☞ making eye contact and keeping an open posture
  - ☞ encouraging other people to state their opinion in their own words
  - ☞ clarifying to make sure you understand the other person's perspective
  - ☞ restating or summarizing the problem to make sure you are on the same page
  - ☞ reflecting and showing that you understand how the other person is feeling

Discussion Questions
- Do you know someone who is the Dodger? What does he or she do to avoid confrontation? How do you think he or she feels when someone picks an argument with him or her?
- Do you offer your opinions during class discussions? How does it feel when you speak up in class? Does everyone feel the same way? Why might some people avoid giving their opinions in class?
- Why would someone choose to avoid an argument rather than telling someone else how they feel? Explain your thinking.
- Do you have friends or family members that never disagree with you or anyone else? What is it like to talk with to them? Do you ever get frustrated that they do not stand up for themselves?
- Do you feel comfortable voicing your opinion if you disagree with someone? Why or why not?
- What might you do if you express an opinion and the other person insists that they are right without really hearing you? How could you avoid a confrontation without fighting back or giving up?
- How might you tell if someone is agreeing with you just to avoid an argument or if he or she actually shares your opinion?

Teaching Activities

I = Individual   P = Pair   G = Group

Section	Subject Area	Activities
pp. 20–21	Language Arts/ The Arts (visual) (I)	Have students read and discuss the "Do's and Don'ts" section. Ask them if they can add any more tips to this list. Have each student create a PowerPoint® presentation to encourage other students to follow these tips to deal with confrontation in a positive way. Encourage students to enhance their presentations with photos, sound effects, or even short video clips. Have them present their slideshows to the class.
pp. 20–21	Language Arts/ The Arts (visual) (I/G)	Have students create brochures, flyers, or bookmarks to illustrate the "Do's and Don'ts." Ask students where they think the best places would be to display their brochures to make sure their message reaches as many students as possible. Make copies of their brochures and place them in these locations.
pp. 22–25	The Arts (drama)/ Guidance and Career Education (P)	Have students work in pairs to choose one of the situations in the quiz to role-play for the class. Ask each pair to demonstrate two perspectives on the situations: the first one illustrates a mishandled situation, and the second one shows how the situation could be handled in a more constructive manner. After each play, discuss the results with the class.
pp. 22–25	Language Arts/ The Arts (drama) (I)	Have students work in small groups to take the quiz. Encourage them to think about how the different characters might feel during the situations. Have them choose one of the scenarios and write a dialogue in which one of the characters attempts to resolve the conflict without an argument. Students may wish to act out their dialogues for the class.
pp. 22–25	Language Arts/ Mathematics (I/G)	Have students use the quiz questions as the basis for a survey. Ask them to add a fourth option, so that the respondents can offer their own solutions. Have each student survey at least three people from outside their classroom. Once they have their surveys complete, ask them to compile their data in a spreadsheet for analysis and graphing. Have them present their findings and discuss them as a class.
pp. 26–27	The Arts (drama)/ Guidance and Career Education (I/G)	Have students brainstorm situations that could result in an argument. Write down the students' suggestions on pieces of paper and have students randomly choose one and act it out. Ask students to volunteer suggestions on how they might resolve the situation before it turns into an argument.
pp. 26–27	Language Arts/ Canada and World Studies (I)	Have students research to find out about famous pacifists, such as Mahatma Ghandi, Leo Tolstoy, Martin Luther King Jr., Te Whiti-o-Rongomai, or Thich Nhat Hanh. Ask them to write a short biography of their pacifist and what actions he or she took to change other people's thinking. Encourage them to include a list of strategies that their pacifist used that other students could apply to other situations to resolve conflict in a positive way and avoid arguments.

The Peacemaker

Highlights
- The Peacemaker is a witness to arguing who has the opportunity to help mediate the situation.
- Effective Peacemakers see conflict as an opportunity to improve relationships, find solutions, and make sure everyone's needs are met.
- You can be an effective Peacemaker by:
    - ☛ setting a good example for others by treating people with respect
    - ☛ helping people who are arguing to calm down
    - ☛ being an empathetic listener and offering support
    - ☛ trying to identify the problem and the emotions behind it
    - ☛ offering lots of solutions and trying to find a compromise that works for everyone

Discussion Questions
- How would you define peacemaker? What do you think are some of the qualities of a Peacemaker? Explain your thinking.
- Do you know anyone who seems to be a Peacemaker? What makes him or her a Peacemaker? Give some examples of behaviour that you have seen that would belong to a Peacemaker.
- Do you think that everyone has to choose to be a Peacemaker, a Dodger, or a Challenger all the time? Why or why not? What other options do you have to avoid arguments?
- Is it possible to have every conflict resolved by a Peacemaker? Which types of situations might require a Peacemaker? In which types of situations might a Peacemaker not help resolve the issue?
- Would you like to be a Peacemaker? Why or why not? How might being a Peacemaker help you at home, school, or work?
- Do you think that anyone could learn to be a Peacemaker? How might they achieve this?
- Can you think of any famous Peacemakers? (e.g., Lester B. Pearson, Martin Luther King, Mahatma Gandhi, Nelson Mandela) What did they do to help resolve conflict?

Teaching Activities

I = Individual   P = Pair   G = Group

Section	Subject Area	Activities
pp. 28–29	Language Arts / Guidance and Career Education (G)	Have students work in small groups to find out about peer mediation or conflict resolution programs that are available in their school or community. Ask students to create a flyer or brochure to tell other students about these programs and how they can get involved. Encourage students to present their findings to other classes.
pp. 28–29	Social Studies/ Media Literacy (I/G)	Play the Peacemaker Radio Minute from Histori.ca for students. Ask them to think about how the producer used the dialogue to establish the situation and explain the history. Have students listen to it again and see if the Peacemaker in the Radio Minute followed the "Do's and Don'ts" on p. 29. If time permits, have students script their own Radio Minute dramatizing a situation in which a Peacemaker uses the "Do's and Don'ts" to help resolve an argument.
pp. 30–31	Language Arts (G)	Point out to students the first bullet in the "Did You Know?" section. Divide the class into two groups and have them debate the statement: Disagreements are the same as arguments. Give students time to discuss and establish their position and then have the two groups debate the issue. When they are finished, encourage students to discuss what techniques they used to express their opinions without getting angry and resorting to arguing.
pp. 30–31	Language Arts/ Guidance and Career Education (I/G)	Have students write a journal entry about how a Peacemaker might resolve a situation. Ask students to think of a situation that might result in an argument, using the ones presented in the quiz as a starting point. Have them write out steps on how they would make sure they understood both sides of the issues and then brainstorm a list of possible solutions that would work for everyone involved. Encourage students to use this entry as a reference when they find themselves in conflict situations.

Bullying:
Deal with it before push comes to shove

Almost everyone has felt bullied at one point in his or her life. Bullying is when someone purposely seeks to scare or hurt another person. Bullying tends to occur repeatedly. It can have negative, long-lasting effects on the person who is bullied, as well as those around the bully and the victim. *Bullying: Deal with it before push comes to shove* was created to give students suggestions on how to handle diverse situations in which they may experience bullying directly (i.e., being bullied themselves) or indirectly (i.e., seeing others being bullied).

In this resource guide, teachers are given valuable discussion topics and activities to help students as they read *Bullying*. In order to get the most out of your class discussions and activities, it is important to create an open atmosphere and a positive classroom community. Building trust and amity within the classroom, by allowing students to openly voice questions and concerns about everyday issues, will create an atmosphere of support and understanding. It is within this context that rich discussions can unfold and help students identify their values and strengths. In turn, this confidence in their own beliefs will empower them to make conscious, responsible decisions.

Before You Begin

Here are some tips and suggestions to help you plan your bullying unit:

- Gather as much material as you can about bullying, including *Bullying: Deal with it before push comes to shove*. (See More Help on page 32 of *Bullying* for a listing of materials.)
- Consider using *Cyberbullying: Deal with it and ctrl alt delete it* in conjunction with this unit, or as a follow-up to this unit.
- Speak to your principal about implementing a whole-school bullying initiative to help all students recognize incidents of bullying and take steps to prevent it.
- Prepare a classroom bulletin board to display posters, pictures, words, and, as the theme develops, your students' work.
- Determine the amount of teaching time you will spend on the bullying unit and integrate the activities into various subject areas to help maximize teaching time.
- Include videos to help stimulate conversations by giving students something objective to discuss, rather than asking them to share personal experiences. Preview videos to ensure that the content is appropriate for your students' age and maturity level.
- You may wish to inform parents that you will be discussing the topic of bullying in the classroom. Encourage them to follow-up with discussion at home to ensure that students feel safe and confident to talk to them about situations they witness or are involved in.
- Note that *Bullying: Deal with it before push comes to shove* includes a variety of sensitive issues and situations (e.g., physical, sexual, emotional, and racial bullying) that are important to address, but may not be appropriate for all grade levels. It is important that teachers preview the book to select material and content that is appropriate for their student's maturity level.

Bullying 101

Highlights

- Bullying is when someone frightens or hurts another person deliberately (on purpose) and repeatedly (again and again).
- The three basic types of bullying are:
  - physical
  - verbal
  - emotional
- Bullying may be:
  - direct (e.g., physical contact, teasing, taking items from the victim)
  - indirect (e.g., gossiping, leaving people out of social settings, using derogatory comments about races, religions, gender, sexual orientation)

Discussion Questions

- What does bullying look like? What words or actions might you see when bullying is happening?
- Have you ever seen someone being bullied? Have you ever seen a bullying act on a television show? Who was being bullied? Who was the bully?
- What happens to people who are bullied? How do you think a bullied person feels?
- How would you describe a bully? Can we tell who is a bully just by looking at him or her? (NOTE: Discussions should lead to the idea that bullies are not always physically bigger or stronger than their victims. Rather, a bully can be anyone who uses his or her power to make someone else feel inferior.)
- What is the difference between bullying and teasing? How do you feel when someone teases you?
- Does bullying happen in your school? What types of bullying happen in your school? Where does bullying take place in your school or in your community?
- Do you think that bullying is accepted in our society? What role should parents and peers play in bullying situations?
- How do the media (television, the Internet, music videos, commercials) play a role in bullying? Do you think it encourages or discourages bullying acts? Why?

Teaching Activities

I = Individual   P = Pair   G = Group

Section	Subject Area	Activities
pp. 2–5	Social Studies/ Language Arts/ Mathematics (G)	Have students work in groups to brainstorm examples of bullying. Ask them to create a Venn diagram to sort their examples into direct and/or indirect forms of bullying, and to indicate which type of bullying (e.g., physical, social, emotional, etc.) their examples represent. Encourage students to display and explain their charts to the class.
pp. 2–5	Social Responsibility/ Language Arts (G)	Have students work in small groups to think about situations in which people might be bullied at school. Have them brainstorm ideas on how they might deal with each of the situations in a positive way. After students have shared their ideas, ask each group to write a contract for acceptable behavior. Bring groups together and invite them to share their ideas to create a class contract for acceptable behaviour.
pp. 4–5	The Arts (drama) (G)	Students work in small groups to create tableaus illustrating the different forms that bullying might take. Encourage students to think about how they can convey the emotion of each situation using their body language, facial expressions, and simple props. During each tableau, invite students in the audience to identify the type of bullying taking place and how they think each person in the tableau might feel during the scene.
pp. 6–7	Language Arts (I)	Have students choose one of the comic strips. Ask them to write a persuasive letter to the school principal, convincing him or her to take action on bullying. In their letters, students should explain the situation and suggest solutions on how to prevent this form of bullying from taking place.
pp. 8–9	Language Arts (G)	Divide students into groups of two or three. Give each group one of the quiz scenarios. As a group, students read the scenario, decide whether or not it is an example of bullying, and why they think so. Have each group present their scenario and decision to the class, encouraging other groups to discuss their presentation.
pp. 10–11	Language Arts/ Media Literacy (I)	Have students create a "Dear Bully Counsellor" message board in the classroom. Ask each student to anonymously write to the Bully Counsellor, asking for advice on a situation (either real or imagined). Have them post their messages on the board. Students then choose a message (not their own) from the board and write a response to it, indicating why the bullying behaviour is inappropriate and some advice on how to deal with the situation.
pp. 12–13	Media Literacy/ The Arts (visual) (I)	Ask students to look for images that depict different forms of bullying. Have them use these images to create posters that encourage people to take a stand against bullying. Encourage students to include a slogan to help get their message across (e.g., Just Say No To Bullying). Display posters around your classroom and/or school.

The Target

Highlights

- The Bully may pick their Target for any number of reasons. They often choose someone who is:
  - ☛ really nice, because they are easier to pick on or scare
  - ☛ perceived to be different in some way (e.g., smaller, heavier, weaker, younger, less assertive, has a physical or learning disability, or is of a different race, nationality, religion, sexual orientation)
- Targets should remember that there is nothing wrong with them — it is the bullies who may feel bad about themselves or angry about something. Bullies look for someone to pick on to make themselves feel better.
- Targets can help themselves by:
  - ☛ being assertive when they speak with a bully
  - ☛ seeking assistance from a parent, teacher, or trustworthy adult
  - ☛ staying with friends (there is safety in numbers)
  - ☛ not trying to solve the situation on their own
  - ☛ not blaming themselves

Discussion Questions

- Have you ever been in situations where you felt bullied? What did you do? What steps did you take to help yourself?
- Who are the people in your school and/or community that you can ask for help if you are feeling bullied?
- Think about the different ways you can respond to a bully — passively, assertively, or aggressively. What is positive about each response? In which situations might these responses work best? Are there times when these responses might not be appropriate?
- Research indicates that Targets often report low self-esteem. Why do you think Targets might feel badly about themselves? What are some ways in which a Target might develop better self-esteem?
- "Bullying is just a normal, unavoidable part of life. Being bullied builds character." Do you agree or disagree with this statement? Explain your thinking. Why do you think someone might say this?
- Is there anything that peers can do to help in bullying situations?
- How do you think schools might help those who are targeted by bullies? What does your school do well to combat bullying? What other strategies would you like to see your school put in place?

Teaching Activities

I = Individual   P = Pair   G = Group

Section	Subject Area	Activities
pp. 14–15	Social Studies (G)	NOTE: This activity requires some prep work. Generate a list of five to ten examples of bullying in the form of "Cross the line if…" statements (e.g., "Cross the line if you have ever been made fun of for wearing glasses." Or, "Cross the line if you or someone you know has ever been pushed or shoved on purpose."). To begin the activity, put a piece of masking tape along the floor. Have students stand in a straight line, side-by-side, with feet touching the line. Tell students that this is a silent activity. Read off the "Cross the line if…" statements one at a time. Students step over the line if the statement applies to them. Continue reading statements until most or all of the students have stepped over the line. Ask students to return to their seats and discuss the activity. Encourage them to think about how many of the examples applied to them and how bullying affects everyone.
pp. 16–17	Language Arts (I)	Have students draw a chart with the headings "Passive," "Assertive," and "Aggressive" down the left side and "Definition," "Examples," "Pros," and "Cons" along the top. Ask them to fill out the chart. When they are finished, encourage students to share and discuss their charts with other classmates.
pp. 16–17	Language Arts (P/G)	Divide students into pairs or small groups. Give each group one of the scenarios from the quiz and ask them to discuss how they would respond to the situation (e.g., passively, assertively, and aggressively) and why. When they are finished, have two groups share their scenarios and discussions.
pp. 18–19	Language Arts (I)	Write the following sentence starters on the board: • I have experienced bullying when… • The bully made me feel… • Places in my school/community where I feel safe… • Places in my school/community where I don't feel safe… • If I were bullied, some of the strategies I would use are… Have students use these sentence starters to write a journal entry about being the Target.
pp. 18–19	Science/Health and Physical Education/The Arts (visual) (I)	Ask students to review the "Did You Know?" section. Have them research to find out more about these facts and how people can help prevent health problems by dealing with negative feelings in a positive way. Have students use their findings to create a poster, brochure, or slideshow to give other students tips on how to manage their feelings and avoid health problems.
pp. 18–19	Health and Physical Education/ Language Arts (G)	Divide the class into groups of boys and girls. You may wish to have the groups work in different areas of the classroom to give students a more comfortable climate in which to share their ideas and experiences. Lead focus-group discussions on the topic of "sexual bullying." You may choose to begin the discussion with a topic statement, such as: "It is normal for boys to tease girls when girls dress provocatively."

21

The Bully

Highlights

- The bully is someone who:
    - ☛ may have been bullied
    - ☛ may not be able to deal well with feelings of anger, sadness, etc.
    - ☛ may have poor self-esteem and want others to feel the same way
    - ☛ may like to show off and get attention from audiences
- Engaging in bullying behaviours as a young person may lead to problems as an adult, such as crime, drug/alcohol abuse, spousal and/or child abuse, and trouble in jobs and relationships.
- Bullies can change their behaviours by:
    - ☛ talking about their own issues and feelings
    - ☛ learning strategies to deal with anger and frustration in appropriate ways
    - ☛ walking away from situations in which they feel challenged
    - ☛ asking for help to change behaviours
    - ☛ joining positive social groups
    - ☛ apologizing to Targets and demonstrating new respect
    - ☛ praising themselves for good choices

Discussion Questions

- Describe a time when you said or did something that hurt another person. Did you do this on purpose? Why? How did you feel about the situation?
- Have you ever been involved in a situation when a group of your friends was picking on, making inappropriate comments about, or isolating another person? Why did your group decide to do that? How did it make you feel?
- Are there times when it is okay to pick on another person? When or why?
- Do you find it hard to control your temper sometimes? What do you do when someone makes you angry or hurts you?
- Who are the people in your school and/or community that you can ask for help if you are feeling angry or frustrated?
- Do you think that boys and girls experience the same types of bullying? How might male and female bullies act differently towards their Targets?
- What does your school do to help bullies modify their behaviours? How might bullies go about changing their behaviours in your school and/or community? What information is available to help bullies make changes to their own behaviours? Who can help?

Teaching Activities

I = Individual   P = Pair   G = Group

Section	Subject Area	Activities
pp. 20–21	The Arts (visual) (I)	Have students create a collage coat of arms for themselves using a variety of materials. Their coat of arms should have four sections, each representing different aspects of their personalities. Encourage students to think about the following as they create their crests: • Things I am interested in and/or do well • Things I admire about others • Things I would like to be better at • Words I would like people to use to describe me When they are finished, have students present them to the class and discuss how being more self-aware and taking pride in yourself could help prevent you from becoming the Target.
pp. 20–21	Media Literacy (G)	Have students work in small groups to create a magazine ad for bullying-prevention services that Dr. Shrink-Wrapped might offer to bullies seeking to change their behaviours. Encourage them to think about their target audience and how they might appeal to them.
pp. 22–23	Guidance and Career Education (I)	Have students work independently to complete the quiz. When they are finished, ask them to reflect on the number of statements they identified as true, and to look back over the quiz to see if there is a pattern. Have students write a journal entry about the quiz. Encourage them to think about whether or not they were surprised by some of their answers and how they feel about their score. Ask students to identify a behaviour or attitude they wish to change and describe a strategy they could use to help modify it.
pp. 22–23	Media Literacy (G)	Have students search through teen magazines or websites to find photos and/or advertisements that depict different forms of bullying. Students then repeat the search process, seeking pictures that depict anti-bullying behaviours (e.g., people working side-by-side; positive body language, etc.). Have students work together to create two collages — one depicting negative images of bullying and the other showing images of how to stop or prevent bullying. Display the two collages side-by-side in the classroom.
pp. 24–25	Mathematics (I)	Ask students to look at the survey results across the bottom of the page. Have students create their own survey about bullying in their school. Encourage them to review all the information on pp. 20–25 to help them come up with survey questions. They should poll their classmates as well as other classrooms and grades (if possible). When they have gathered their data, ask students to graph their results and present them to the class.
pp. 24–25	The Arts (drama/music) (I)	Have students review the "Do's and Don'ts" on p. 25. Ask them to write a short poem or rap that helps illustrate how a bully can make better choices about his or her own behaviours. Students could perform their pieces for the class or younger students in the school.

The Witness

Highlights

- Witnesses (also known as bystanders) play an important role in bullying situations. Many Witnesses do not speak up or take action because they:
  - ☛ fear losing friends
  - ☛ may be seen as an informer
  - ☛ fear becoming the bully's next Target
  - ☛ may admire or respect the Bully
  - ☛ may use the Bully as protection and join in on the behaviours
- Witnesses can make a big difference for Targets by:
  - ☛ seeking help from a trustworthy adult on behalf of the victim
  - ☛ setting a good example by treating others with respect
  - ☛ speaking up against bullying
  - ☛ asking the Target what they can do to help him or her
  - ☛ offering the Target support and friendship
  - ☛ discouraging the Bully's actions (e.g., don't take the Bully's side, tell the Bully to stop what he/she is doing) and refusing to hang out with the Bully

Discussion Questions

- Have you ever witnessed someone being bullied by another student? How did you feel during the situation? What did you do during the situation?
- What are some strategies that a Witness might use to change a bullying situation?
- What can you do in your school to help Witnesses who want to change bullying situations? What strategies or ideas should be implemented?
- If you thought a friend was being bullied by a parent or other adult, what might you do to help your friend?
- Should Witnesses always get involved in bullying situations? What are some different ways that a Witness can help the Target?
- Have you every watched a news story about bullying? What were the reporter's feelings about the incident? How could you tell? Did the story tell if the situation was resolved? Would you have told the story differently?

- Recently, people have posted videos of schoolyard fights and other bullying incidents on the Internet. Do you think they should be allowed to post these types of videos? Why or why not? How might people react to seeing these videos? Do you think that this might encourage bullying behaviours?
- Have you ever watched a scene in a movie or on a television show that showed bullying and wished that the characters had made different choices? Describe the situation and what would you have done differently.

Teaching Activities

I = Individual   P = Pair   G = Group

Section	Subject Area	Activities
pp. 26–27	Media Literacy/ The Arts (visual)/ Social Responsibility (I)	Ask students to review the "Do's and Don'ts" on p. 27. Have them create a poster that compares and contrasts the Do's and Don'ts of being a proactive Witness. Students may choose one Do and one Don't to illustrate in side-by-side scenes, or they may create a collection of small scenes.
pp. 26–27	Media Literacy (G)	Encourage students to examine newspapers or the Internet for articles about bullying incidents that involve witnesses. Ask them to think about the roles of the Bully, the Target, and the Witness in the events. Have students work in groups to discuss the Witnesses' choice and what they might have done differently. When they are finished, groups can present their findings to the class.
pp. 28–31	The Arts (drama) (G)	Have students work in small groups to role-play characters in the scenarios described in the quiz. Encourage students to demonstrate one or two ways that the situation could be handled by a Witness as the answers suggest. Students may perform their plays for the class or for younger students.
pp. 28–31	Mathematics (G)	Have students work in small groups to create a survey to find out the types of bullying incidents and where they occur in their school. Ask students to graph the data and use their findings to suggest ways they might make their school safer for students.
pp. 28–31	Language Arts/ The Arts (drama) (I)	Have students choose one of the scenarios in the quiz and write a monologue from the perspective of one of the characters — the Bully, the Target, or the Witness. Students may share their monologues orally in short presentations.

Cliques:
Deal with it using what you have inside

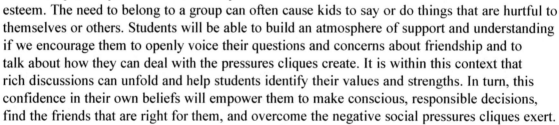

Most of us feel the need to be acknowledged and accepted by different groups around us, however this positive interest can become negative when a group takes the form of a clique. Negative consequences arise when cliques demand that their members give up friendships and values to maintain the acceptance of the clique, or when members fear being rejected if they speak out about their beliefs. *Cliques: Deal with it using what you have inside* was created to give students suggestions on how to handle diverse situations in which their peers may challenge their values.

In this resource guide, teachers are given valuable discussion topics and activities to help students as they read *Cliques*. In order to get the most out of your class discussions and activities, it is important to create an open atmosphere and a positive classroom community. Friendships, positive relationships, and positive activities help build kids' self-esteem. The need to belong to a group can often cause kids to say or do things that are hurtful to themselves or others. Students will be able to build an atmosphere of support and understanding if we encourage them to openly voice their questions and concerns about friendship and to talk about how they can deal with the pressures cliques create. It is within this context that rich discussions can unfold and help students identify their values and strengths. In turn, this confidence in their own beliefs will empower them to make conscious, responsible decisions, find the friends that are right for them, and overcome the negative social pressures cliques exert.

Before You Begin
Here are some tips and suggestions to help you plan your cliques unit:
- Gather as much material as you can about cliques, including *Cliques: Deal with it using what you have inside*. (See More Help on page 32 of *Cliques* for a listing of materials.)
- Decide on the scope of your study, depending on the grade level you teach and the needs of your students.
- Display books for children on this topic. In addition, prepare a bulletin board for posters, pictures, and, as the theme develops, your students' work.
- Decide on the amount of time that you plan to spend on this theme.
- Note that cliques affect students from elementary school through to high school, and even adults. *Cliques: Deal with it using what you have inside* includes a variety of sensitive issues and situations (e.g., cyberbullying, race relations, sexual insults, etc.) that are important to address, but may not be appropriate for all grade levels. It is important that teachers preview the book to select material and content that is appropriate for their students' maturity level.

Cliques 101

Highlights
- Cliques occur when groups of people spend a lot of time together thinking the same way or doing the same things. Cliques exert negative influences because they exclude others or demand people act in certain ways if they want to belong to the clique.
- Cliques can come from a variety of places, including:
    - ☛ special interest groups — sports, music, theatre, "smart" kids
    - ☛ racial groups
    - ☛ in-crowd
    - ☛ neighbourhoods
- Cliques can exert different forms of pressure:
    - ☛ name-calling
    - ☛ ostracism
    - ☛ put-downs
    - ☛ cyberbullying
    - ☛ physical harassment
    - ☛ spreading rumours

Discussion Questions
- Are you a member of an ethnic or racial group, a sports team, club or social group? Does belonging to this group make you feel special or better than others? Why or why not?
- Can being a member of a group boost your self-esteem and give you confidence to do things you wouldn't have thought of or had the courage to do as an individual?
- Name a time when you felt that a group had become a clique. What event triggered that feeling in you? Was it a positive or negative event? What did you do?
- Have you ever felt pressured to dress or act in a certain way to gain the approval of a clique? What happened? How did it make you feel?
- Has belonging to a clique become more important than staying on good terms with your friends and family? How did you rationalize your actions to your friends and family, and to yourself?
- Have you ever done anything that went against your set of values or was illegal, just to keep the approval of a clique? Do you know someone who has? What did you do?
- Have you ever been abandoned by a friend who wanted to join a clique? Did you ever abandon a friend so that you could join a clique?
- Did you ever fall out of favour with a clique and try to regain past friendships? Did it work? What did you learn?
- Do you think you need to belong to a clique to survive in school? Why or why not?
- Have cliques ever caused tension or problems at school or in your personal life? Where did you fit in to this conflict? What did you do?

Teaching Activities

I = Individual   P = Pair   G = Group

Section	Subject Area	Activities
pp. 2-3	Language Arts (G)	Make a T-chart, labelling the columns "Positive" and "Negative." Have students work in small groups to fill in the chart with examples of how groups may be positive and negative. Have students compare and discuss other groups' charts as class.
pp. 4–5	The Arts (drama) (G)	In groups of 3–4, have students make a tableau to show an example of a clique at work (e.g., a clique pressuring a student to "prove" he/she is worthy of belonging, announcing what he/she must do to gain membership). After 8 seconds, have students slowly transform into a new tableau showing a positive example of someone standing up to this behaviour (e.g., a member of the clique refusing to go along with it).
pp. 6–7	The Arts (I)	Have students choose the scenario that they relate to the most and continue the comic to depict a positive outcome.
pp. 6–7	Language Arts (I)	Ask students to write a journal entry or a letter to one of the characters, giving them strategies to use when a clique exerts pressure.
pp. 8–9	Language Arts (G)	Have students choose a question from the quiz. Use a Think-Pair-Share strategy to discuss various responses and ideas on how to how to make belonging to a group positive and inclusive.
pp. 10–11	Language Arts (I)	Using the template of a kid writing to a counsellor, have students write a poem or song about a student who gives up a friend/boyfriend/girlfriend to join a clique. The counsellor can offer advice in poem or song. The end should result in a positive conclusion.
pp. 10–11	Media Literacy (I/G)	Encourage students to think about how to make the dynamics of clique mentality work in a positive way. To start, have students cut out pictures from magazines that depict different types of cliques — the fashionable crowd, the sports jocks — as well as the "ordinary" kids. Have them talk about whether being "in" is just a perception or a reality. Students can work in groups to discuss what they see in the images they have collected.
pp. 12–13	The Arts (drama) (G)	In small groups, students should role-play myth-busting scenarios (e.g., the notion of "in-crowd" and "popularity", loyalty to a racial or ethnic group and other examples from the book). Students can create "sound tableaux" in which they improvise but instead of speaking they use only sound to express their feelings. Encourage groups to present their skits to the class.

The Outsider

Highlights
- The Outsider is the person who is excluded from a clique. He or she might want to join the clique or might be the victim of their cruelty.
- If you feel you are being excluded or bullied by a clique, you can:
    - ☛ think about the values that are important to you
    - ☛ talk to long-time friends or other kids whose opinions you respect
    - ☛ talk to people in the clique about the effect of the clique's pressures or actions
    - ☛ get involved with other people and activities
    - ☛ talk to an adult who might offer advice or assistance

Discussion Questions
- Do you feel you are a "loser" if you don't belong to the "right" crowd? Why or why not?
- How important to you is being accepted by a group or clique? What are you willing to give up just to be part of the in-crowd?
- What are some examples of pressure or controls by a clique?
- Why do you think people might give in to the pressure of a clique? What might be some consequences of giving in to these pressures? Give some examples.
- Imagine being in a situation where a clique wants you to do something that goes against your values or beliefs. How might you handle that pressure?
- Imagine a situation in which you know that a clique has targeted someone else. Give some examples. What could you do to help that person?
- Would you consider acceptance by a clique more important than the disapproval of your family and your old friends?
- What might happen if you say "No" to the clique? What factors might affect your decisions?
- What would you do if you knew people inside a clique were committing harmful or illegal acts? Would you turn to an adult to help stop the negative or dangerous behaviour? Brainstorm a list of people that might help you.
- Do you think you can be happy without belonging to a clique? How can you make your life full of friendships and social activities without belonging to a clique?

Teaching Activities

I = Individual   P = Pair   G = Group

Section	Subject Area	Activities
pp. 14–15	Mathematics (G)	Ask students to survey their classmates to find out their feelings about and experiences with cliques. Have them write 8–10 survey questions, such as: • Have you ever felt pressured by a clique? • Would your life be happier if you were a member of a clique? • What would you do to impress a clique you wanted to join? • Have students display the results in a graph or chart and discuss their findings with the class.
pp. 15	Language Arts (I)	Have students write original letters to "Dear Dr. Shrink-Wrapped" from the perspective of someone who is the victim of an organized campaign by a clique. Have students do a blind exchange of letters and write back as Dr. Shrink-Wrapped about how to solve his/her problem.
pp. 16–17	The Arts (drama) (G)	Have students work in groups of 3–4 to brainstorm a list of scenarios in which they deal with the pressures of a clique (e.g., ridicule, a malicious website, physical threats). Encourage them to review the scenarios presented in the quiz to help them get started. Have students select one scenario and discuss a positive solution to the problem. If possible, have students create a 20-second clay animation recording to show to the class.
pp. 18–19	Language Arts (I/G)	Place posters around the room with the following sentence starters: I believe in… I don't believe in… My friends are… My friends are not… Belonging to a group means… Belonging to a group does not mean… I say "yes" when… I say "no" when… When I'm pressured, I feel… When I feel pressured, I can talk to… Allow 5–10 min for students to write a response to each sentence starter. Afterwards, review the responses with the class to discuss the words, messages and feelings that students have given.

The Insider

Highlights

- The Insider is the person who has "made it" into the clique. The Insider either fears being kicked out of the clique or tries to control how others act. Sometimes an Insider disagrees with the behaviour or actions of the clique but is afraid of saying so for fear of being excluded by people he or she thinks are friends.
- How can you avoid being controlled by a clique?
- Think about the consequences of a clique's negative attitudes or actions. Think about how you would feel if a clique shunned you because you weren't "popular" or compliant to its demands.
- Voice your ideas and concerns to the clique. Don't be intimidated by the threat of excommunication. Be yourself.
- Don't get involved with negative activities, such as name-calling, tagging, vandalism, or cyberbullying.
- Reflect on the groups you belong to and whether or not they treat people in a positive way.
- Take responsibility for the past. Be honest with people who have been hurt by your clique.
- Renew old friendships.
- Volunteer for work that interests you or join a new club and make new friends.

Discussion Questions

- Have you ever felt the need to change your attitude or do something you don't want to do just to gain the approval of a clique? How did it make you feel?
- What are some possible consequences of conforming just to belong to a clique?
- Would you give up old friends just to gain a clique's acceptance?
- Imagine being in a situation where a clique decides to target an "outsider" in a negative way. How could you prevent it? Who can you talk to?
- Do you spread rumours or gossip about old friends or "outsiders" to maintain the clique's acceptance? Would you want to be the target of rumours or gossip?
- Think about a time when you were intimidated or excluded by a clique. How did you feel? Now that you belong, do you enjoy treating others that way?
- Do you feel that only "losers" don't belong to a clique? What's a "winner"? Why?
- What impact can your membership in a clique have on your family life? What if your family disapproves of your clique and its actions?
- What impact can belonging to a clique have on your school life? What's more important to you, "belonging" now or your long-term goals? How can you have both close friendships and your independence? Does being part of a clique make you more popular or happy? Why?
- How can you keep friendships within a group healthy so it won't become a clique?

Teaching Activities

I = Individual P = Pair G = Group

Section	Subject Area	Activities
pp. 20–21	Visual Arts (I/G)	Ask students to choose a "Do" and a "Don't" from the book. Have them use pictures and words to create a poster that contrasts the "Do" with the "Don't." Display and discuss the posters with the class.
pp. 20–21	Media Literacy/ Visual Arts (I/G)	Have students collect images of group/clique/gang behaviour. Display each image and have students indicate which attitude it shows and why they think so. Ask them if they think the image shows someone pressuring or being pressured or included and how it makes them feel. After you have reviewed all of the images, follow up with a discussion about what students might do when they catch themselves displaying the same attitudes.
pp. 22–23	Goal Setting (I/G)	Have students work through the quiz. When they are finished, ask them to look at the statements that they identified as true. Have them think about how they might deal with the insecurities they feel and the negative consequences of trying to "belong." Encourage them to write out ideas that might help them and discuss them as a group. Teachers can revisit these issues and conference with students to discuss their progress throughout the year.
pp. 24–25	Media Literacy (I)	Invite a former gang member to class. Students can interview the individual about the consequences of gang activity on society and the effects of membership on the gang and the members who want to get out.

The Witness

Highlights

- The Witness is the person who sees someone else trying to please a clique or who sees someone being victimized by a clique. The Witness might feel that he or she is not part of the problem, but there may be opportunities to positively influence the situation.
- If you feel someone is being pressured to join a clique or being victimized by a clique, you can:
    - ☛ talk to him/her about the issue and let him/her know he/she could make better choices
    - ☛ let him/her know that you are there to be his/her friend and should not tolerate being victimized
    - ☛ encourage him/her to talk to a trusted adult about what to do

Discussion Questions

- Have you ever seen someone acting out of character or doing the wrong thing just to impress a clique or gang? How were you involved? What did you do?
- What would you be willing to stand up for? Would you seek out a friendship with someone to keep him or her from being targeted by a clique?
- How could you redirect friends you care about from getting in too far with cliques or gangs?
- If one of your friends were committing illegal activities would you report them to his/her parents, the principal or the police?
- Do you think *witness* and *bystander* mean the same thing? How are they the same or different? Explain your answer.
- Would you help a friend cover up for something wrong or illegal he/she has done and regrets? What's the best thing to do to help him/her?
- Have you ever witnessed a clique targeting someone else? What was the situation? How were you involved?
- Would you risk being targeted by a clique to protect or defend another person the clique is victimizing?
- Imagine a friend who shows the stress of being victimized by a clique. How can you help? Should you talk to an adult if you fear the stress is too great?

Teaching Activities

I = Individual   P = Pair   G = Group

Section	Subject Area	Activities
pp.26–27	Media Literacy (I/G)	Have students select one of the "Do's" listed on pp. 27. Ask them to think about how they might encourage other people their age to adapt that strategy to help a friend. Have them create a storyboard for a TV advertisement to promote that strategy. Share the advertisements with the class.
pp. 27	Language Arts (G)	Have students work in small groups to make a board game based on the "Do's" and "Don'ts" presented on pp. 27. When a player throws the dice he or she can only advance by providing an acceptable answer to a real-life problem posed by cards in the middle of the board. Encourage students to share and play their board games with the class.
pp. 28–31	The Arts (drama) (G)	Have students work in groups of 4 to create a skit showing what might happen if a witness chooses not to get involved when he/she sees a friend being targeted by a clique. Then have students create an alternate ending to their skit showing what might happen in the same situation when a witness gets involved in a positive way. Encourage students to present their skits to the class
pp. 28–31	Research and Inquiry (G)	Have students relate issues of poverty/race/class to the development/presence/success of gangs in society. As a class, brainstorm about the causes of gangs and how children/teens can be diverted from gang life. Students can develop major research projects or papers that trace this development at different times in society.
pp. 28–31	Language Arts (G)	Have students write personal journals or poems about how each of them perceives his/her positive contribution to school/friendships/society, and how positive friendships can help them achieve more of his/her positive goals.

Cyberbullying:
Deal with it and ctrl alt delete it

Bullying often reoccurs over time and has a very serious impact on all involved. With the increased use of technology, cyberbullying is becoming commonplace, and it is a phenomenon that children and adults are struggling to understand and prevent. Bullying that takes place in emails, instant messaging, text messaging, online chat rooms, blogs, and bulletin boards can seem impossible to escape. Online, information spreads to a large number of people, and it spreads quickly. *Cyberbullying: Deal with it and ctrl alt delete it* was created to give students suggestions on how to handle diverse situations in which they may bully, be bullied, or see others being bullied online.

The exercises in this resource guide encourage students to communicate with fellow students and trustworthy adults about their attitudes and behaviors online. Activities are designed to help students understand that cyberbullying is wrong and that it can be stopped. They also encourage students to educate others, including their own parents, on how to stop cyberbullying.

Before You Begin
Here are some tips and suggestions to help you plan your cyberbullying unit.
- Gather as much material as you can about cyberbullying, including *Cyberbullying: Deal with it and ctrl alt delete it* (See More Help on page 32 of *Cyberbullying* for a listing of materials.)
- Consider supplementing this unit or using it in conjunction with *Bullying: Deal with it before push comes to shove, Privacy: Deal with it like nobody's business,* and *Gossip: Deal with it before word gets around.* See the guides to these topics for related discussion question and teaching activity ideas.
- Decide on the scope of your study, depending on the grade level you teach and the needs of your students. The students' experiences will shape the amount of teaching time spent on this topic.
- Arrange for computer lab time in your school to adequately allow students time to work on various activities.
- Display books for children on this topic. In addition, prepare a bulletin board for posters, pictures, and, as the theme develops, your students' work.
- Encourage the whole school to get involved in this topic. Work with your school librarian, technology specialists, administrators, and school councils to create a safe school environment that is proactive in its approach to safe Internet use and cyberbullying.
- Understand that students may find it difficult to talk with their classmates about personal situations where they have been bullied. Include videos to help stimulate conversations by giving students something objective to discuss, rather than asking them to share personal experiences. Preview videos to ensure that the content is appropriate for your students' age and maturity level. Create a supportive environment and let students know that they have sources of support in the school for issues that they do not feel comfortable sharing in the classroom environment.
- Note that *Cyberbullying: Deal with it and ctrl alt delete it* includes a variety of sensitive issues and situations that are important to address, but may not be appropriate for all grade levels. It is important that teachers preview the book to select material and content that is appropriate for their student's maturity level.

Cyberbullying 101

Highlights
- Acts of bullying may include:
  - 🖝 name calling
  - 🖝 spreading rumours
  - 🖝 making threats
  - 🖝 taking someone's property
  - 🖝 making inappropriate, hurtful comments
- It is bullying regardless of whether it's face to face, or online.
- Cyberbullies use technology to bully others through:
  - 🖝 creating hate or rumour-filled sites
  - 🖝 changing photos of people to embarrass them
  - 🖝 pretending to be someone else and using their identity to hurt others
  - 🖝 asking others to ignore or block someone
  - 🖝 sending files that harm another's computer
- Cyberbullies may bully to entertain, to exclude others, to get revenge, or to scare.

Discussion Questions
- What is bullying? What does it look like face to face? Have you ever experienced a bullying situation?
- What is cyberbullying? What does it look like? Who gets cyberbullied? Have you ever experienced bullying online?
- Do you think cyberbullying is as serious as face-to-face bullying? Why or why not? Do you think cyberbullying has the same effects on the victim as face-to-face bullying? How might the victim feel after being bullied online?
- What is the difference between gossiping online and cyberbullying? What behaviours are acceptable and what are not? Where do you draw the line?
- Which sites do you feel safe using? Have you ever been on a website where you felt unsafe, and if so, what did you do?
- Do you speak with your parents about the sites you visit? Why or why not? Where is your computer located in your house? How could changing the location of your computer at home make you feel safer?
- Do you know your school board's policies on cyberbullying? Is cyberbullying illegal? How do you know if bullying that you are experiencing, or are doing to others, is against the law? Where can you go for more information?

Teaching Activities

I = Individual   P = Pair   G = Group

Section	Subject Area	Activities
pp. 2–5	Language Arts (I/G)	Ask students to write a short paragraph about a situation from their own lives in which they have been either bullied face to face or cyberbullied. Write their stories on the blackboard anonymously and have the class sort them into two categories: "face-to-face bullying" and "cyberbullying." Discuss the similarities and differences in the stories, bullies and cyberbullies, and the victims' feelings.
pp. 6–7	Media Literacy (G)	Have students watch one film or several short videos on cyberbullying (see the Resources in Cyberbullying and in this guide for suggestions). Ask them to discuss as a group how these are examples of using cyberbullying to entertain, to scare, to exclude, or get revenge. Ask them whether the characters in the videos made them think differently about the stereotypical Bully and the stereotypical Target. Have them write a script for a 3-minute film on how cyberbullying is used for these purposes, and have them present the scripts to the class.
pp. 8–9	Language Arts (P/G)	Have students work in pairs to create a Concept Map in which they brainstorm examples of cyberbullying (e.g. a blog with rude comments about a classmate) and examples of online conflicts that are not cyberbullying (e.g. getting kicked off a site by a moderator for using inappropriate language.) Discuss, in pairs and then as a class, any examples that are hard to categorize.
pp. 10–11	Mathematics/ Media Literacy (G)	Using an online survey site such as SurveyMonkey, have students create a survey that asks other students about what types of cyberbullying they have witnessed or experienced themselves. Students from other classes could be asked to complete the online survey. As a class, read and analyze the results. What types of cyberbullying are commonly being experienced by students in your school? Did the data indicate anything of particular interest or concern?
pp. 10–11	Language Arts/ The Arts (visual) (G)	Using the results from any of the above activities, have students work in groups to create posters for display in the computer lab. The posters should indicate types of cyberbullying that are frequently experienced by students and provide tips for dealing with these situations.
pp. 12–13	Social Responsibility/ Media Literacy (I/G)	Ask students to research newspaper articles about incidents of cyberbullying in their city, province, or country. Have them write an opinion piece about their found article discussing the details of the incident and whether or not they agree with the consequences given to the bully (if consequences are indicated) and what they think the appropriate consequences should be.
pp. 12–13	Canada and World Studies/ Media Literacy (P/G)	Ask students to work in pairs to search online for more information about Canadian laws on Internet privacy and cyberbullying (such as Bill 81 and Bill 212). Conduct a follow-up discussion for students to share their results with each other.

Cyberbullying

The Target

Highlights
- A Target may be someone that the bully feels is:
    - popular or happy, and this intimidates the bully
    - different (differences may be physical, or based on interests, beliefs, etc.)
    - part of a group that is seen as weak and easy to target
- Targets should report incidents of cyberbullying to trusted adults and online site moderators.
- They do not have to go through this alone.
- Targets who have experienced cyberbullying in the past should surf only with people they trust who will help them if situations of bullying occur.
- Targets should not attempt to "bully" back. This may aggravate the situation.
- All Internet users should keep personal information private and confidential. Never share passwords, addresses, etc.

Discussion Questions
- How often do you use sites that have a moderator? How often do you use sites that do not have a moderator? What are the advantages of a site moderator?
- Are you aware of the "Terms of Agreement" on any of the sites you use? How would you go about finding this information?
- What strategies do you use to keep your identity private online?
- What do you do when you receive information from someone you don't recognize?
- When a Target is bullied, it effects their self-esteem. What can a Target do to increase his or her self-esteem? Discuss ideas for things a Target can do to reclaim a positive self image. Suggest the idea of having them write down a positive thought about themselves every time they have a negative thought and encourage students to do this throughout the unit.
- Discuss how telling someone and getting help can raise the Target's self-esteem. Discuss how sharing their story can help a Target and help others. What are some ways that a Target can share his or her story?
- What advice would you give to a friend if you knew they were being cyberbullied? Has anyone ever given you helpful bullying advice that you would like to share?

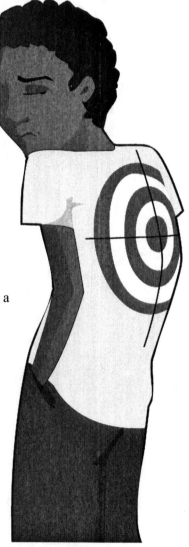

Teaching Activities

I = Individual   P = Pair   G = Group

Section	Subject Area	Activities
pp. 14–15	Language Arts (G)	Students are asked to work in small groups to create a simple oral presentation for students in a younger grade (e.g. primary or junior level) that includes safety information they should know about using the Internet. Students should refer to and include the "Dos and Don'ts" on the double page spread. Book presentation times for groups to visit other classrooms in the school to present their information.
pp. 14–15	Language Arts/ Media Literacy (G)	Ask students to brainstorm as a class the characteristics of a stereotypical Target. Encourage them to think of the examples in the book and discuss how kids from every social group, with any interests, any style, could be a victim of cyberbullying.
pp. 16–17	Language Arts (I/G)	Ask the students to complete the quiz on the double-page spread independently. Ask the students to discuss their answers in small groups, and then discuss the trends they noticed in their answers. Are they more likely to stand up to bullying situations, leave an inappropriate situation, or allow themselves to be bullied? Ask students to discuss what they can do to better handle such situations, and to write down their own answers on a bookmark that they can refer to at any time.
pp. 16–17	Language Arts/ Media Literacy (I/G)	Present the following situation to the students: "You are part of a social networking site that meets often online to discuss the plot of your favourite television series. Usually everyone is very friendly on the site and uses appropriate language and follows net courtesy. Then one evening a new member joins the site and quickly becomes argumentative and rude in their comments. There is a moderator for the site, but the moderator does not appear to be asking the new member to adjust his/ her behaviours. Some of your online friends are considering abandoning the site, but you have always enjoyed the site and do not want to leave it." Have them compose an email message that they could send to the moderator of the site asking them to deal with the situation. Discuss the students' messages as a group.
pp. 18–19	Language Arts/ Social Responsibility (G)	As a class, read and discuss the school's current code of conduct/ discipline policy and identify what the consequences are for incidents of cyberbullying. Ask students if they agree with the consequences stated, and/or if there is a need for further development of a specific cyberbullying policy to be created. If the class agrees that there is a need for a new policy, encourage students to brainstorm ideas that could be presented to school administrators and have them submit or present their ideas.
pp. 18–19	Language Arts/ Technology (G)	Help the students create a Web 2.0 tool (e.g. a bulletin board, threaded discussion etc.) linked to the school's website that allows for incidences of cyberbullying to be reported to school staff.

Cyberbullying

The Bully

Highlights
- Bullies may pick on others for a variety of "reasons." They may:
  - have been bullied themselves
  - feel bad about themselves and want others to feel the same way
  - have an "audience" that encourages bullying behaviour
  - be following the actions of the crowd they are hanging around with
  - not have a "reason." They may just think that it is fun, and that no harm will come of it
- Bullies should be aware of the consequences of their actions, and realize that without help, behaviours can escalate.
- Bullies should seek help from a trusted adult to help change their behaviours.
- It is important to trust our own instincts and not "go along" with friends who are making poor choices, such as bullying another person.

Discussion Questions
- Have you ever spread a rumour online, participated in a "rating" game, or deliberately blocked someone on a chat site to be hurtful? How did you feel about doing this? How do you think the "target" felt?
- Who would you seek help from if you felt your actions online could become bullying?
- Statistics show that 60% of boys who bully in school have criminal records later on in life. Why do you think that this is such a common occurrence? How does bullying behaviour predict more severe behaviours in the future?
- Would you feel safer cyberbullying than bullying in real life? What consequences are you aware of that cyberbullies have received at school or at home for their behaviours? What consequences do face-to-face bullies receive?

- Think about some of your favourite television shows and movies. Have any of the plotlines included cyberbullying? Did the show/movie glamorize, or normalize the behaviours in its depiction? Did it include consequences for the bully?
- What are some strategies you have used in the past to stop yourself from sending messages that could be perceived as cyberbullying? Have you learned any new strategies through our class discussions? What would you do to stop yourself in the future if you ever wanted to cyberbully someone?

Teaching Activities

I = Individual   P = Pair   G = Group

Section	Subject Area	Activities
pp. 20–21	The Arts (visual) (I)	Ask students to create posters depicting some of the characteristics of a "cyberbully" in order to create awareness around what behaviours are considered bullying online (e.g. spreading rumours, blocking someone from participating in a chatroom, encouraging others to make inappropriate comments about a person).
pp. 22–23	Language Arts/ Media Literacy (I)	Upon completion of the quiz, ask students to reflect on their results and then write a journal entry about what they have learned about themselves. Were they surprised or disappointed by anything they learned? What behaviours may they need to change about their online choices?
pp. 22–23	Language Arts (I)	Have students write an apology letter, either to someone that they have bullied in the past, or to themselves from the point of view of a bully who has harassed them in the past. Encourage students to reach out to someone that they have bullied and to apologize.
pp. 22–23	The Arts (drama) (G)	In small groups of 4 or 5, students are asked to create a short role play that depicts a case of cyberbullying on a familiar website. Students should be encouraged to set the scene of the incident, and then address what the next steps should be for the Target and the Bully (e.g. how both people should seek help and from whom). The skits could be presented to other classrooms, or in an assembly.
pp. 24–25	Language Arts/ Media Literacy (G)	Have students work in small groups to create lists of commonly used abbreviations in instant messaging and cell phone messaging. Ask students to sort their lists into two categories: 1) "safe and appropriate" and 2) "unsafe and inappropriate" abbreviations. Students may find they will have a third list of abbreviations that are easily confused, or misunderstood. Ask them to list such terms in a third category and discuss how hurtful these terms can be and what they can do to avoid hurting others through their use. Then have them brainstorm alternatives to the abbreviations that are inappropriate and cross off the inappropriate terms and replace them with appropriate ones.
pp. 24–25	Language Arts/ Social Responsibility (G)	As a whole class, brainstorm a list of professionals (e.g. guidance counselors, police officers, etc.) who may work with students who are bullies, and discuss with them the ways that these professionals can help. As an extension, arrange opportunities for some of the professionals to come into the classroom and participate in a round-table discussion in which the groups can ask questions.

Cyberbullying

The Bystander

Highlights

- Bystanders may feel afraid to speak up because:
  - ☛ they are afraid of attracting the cyberbully's attention
  - ☛ they are worried it may make the situation worse for the target and/or for others
  - ☛ they may be accused of being a "rat" or tattle-tale
  - ☛ they may be afraid of getting blocked or banned from groups or websites
- Bystanders have the power to help others in a variety of ways. They:
  - ☛ can speak up about situations if they feel safe enough to do so
  - ☛ can seek adult assistance to help the target
  - ☛ can be a friend and be supportive to the target
  - ☛ should avoid joining in on the bullying behaviours or encouraging it

Discussion Questions

- Would you let a friend be bullied in real life? What would you do if a bully came face to face and threatened a friend? What would you do if this happened online?
- Have you ever read false information online about someone you know? Did you tell the person who was involved? Did you correct the false information? What would you do differently now?
- How can a bystander encourage bullying behaviour? What are some ways that a bystander can avoid joining in?
- Do you think that schools have a responsibility to have policies in place to deal with incidents of cyberbullying? Why or why not?
- Do you think that parents are ultimately responsible for the choices their kids make online? At what age do you think that kids should be held completely responsible for their own behaviour?
- Do you think that school boards should allow access to all websites (e.g. Facebook, My Space, MSN Messenger)? Why do you think that some boards block these sites? Why do some school boards allow student access to the sites from schools?
- Does watching a video of a schoolyard fight on the Internet make you part of the problem? How would watching such a video encourage the bully? Does visiting celebrity gossip websites encourage bullying?

Teaching Activities

I = Individual   P = Pair   G = Group

Section	Subject Area	Activities
pp. 26–27	Language Arts (G)	Create a "Help the Bystander" bulletin board in the classroom. Students are asked to reflect on an experience in which they have been a witness to a cyberbullying incident, and are asked to write down their incident on paper and post it on the wall anonymously. Students then choose another person's posting to read and create a response to, that includes suggestions about how the bystander could have helped out the target in the situation. The incidents and proposed solutions could be shared aloud upon completion.
pp. 26–27	Language Arts (G)	Have students work in small groups to create a Cyberbullying Tip Sheet for parents with 10 tips to help kids who are Targets, Bullies and Bystanders. Have students take the tip sheets home and encourage them to talk about the tips with their parents.
pp. 28–31	Language Arts (I/G)	As a class, discuss the responsibilities that Bystanders have to stop cyberbullying. Brainstorm ways that people can help prevent cyberbullying before it starts. Have students write an article for their student newspaper on the importance of the Bystander's actions. Encourage students to submit their articles and talk to the school paper about a special cyberbullying issue.
pp. 28–31	Language Arts (P)	Present the statistic "74% of teachers have heard about more than one incident of cyberbullying" to the class. Ask students to work in partners and choose a staff member to conduct a mini-interview with. They should ask the teacher to reflect on any incidents of cyberbullying they have heard about, and what strategies they have used and plan to use in order to help students. As a class, have students create a list of strategies that teachers can use to help students, and create a display for teachers in the staffroom.
pp. 28–31	Language Arts/ Media Literacy (G)	As a class, have students create an online bulletin board where students can post up-to-date articles, podcasts, book reviews, and links about cyberbullying to share with each other and with invited guests to the site. As a class, create a "terms of use" agreement that all students will agree to abide by when using the site. Encourage the students to visit often, and to share their own ideas. Ask for volunteers to help you monitor the site.

Fighting:
Deal with it without coming to blows

All of us have aggressive feelings at one time or another, but fighting is never the right way to solve our problems. As we get older, we need to find ways to accept our aggressive feelings and make smart choices to solve problems in a positive way. *Fighting: Deal with it without coming to blows* gives students suggestions on how to handle diverse situations and deal with issues without fighting.

This resource guide provides a variety of situations in which young people may find themselves, and offers suggestions on how they can deal with their problems without resorting to aggressive behaviour. As you work through the different sections of *Fighting*, encourage students to think about their own experiences and how they can apply the strategies in their own lives. Giving students the tools to deal with fighting and aggression in a positive way will help empower them to make smart choices.

Before You Begin
Here are some tips and suggestions to help you plan your fighting unit:
- Gather as much material as you can about fighting, including *Fighting: Deal with it without coming to blows*. (See More Help on page 32 of *Fighting* for a listing of materials.)
- Decide on the scope of your study, depending on the grade level you teach and the needs of your students.
- You may wish to post tips on peer mediation in your classroom and use them during your discussion of *Fighting*.
- Display books for children on this topic. In addition, prepare a bulletin board for posters, pictures, and, as the theme develops, your students' work.
- Decide on the amount of time that you plan to spend on this theme.
- To ensure sensitivity to home and school issues that might impact your students, please take the time to find out as much as possible about their interpersonal relationships before addressing the subject of fighting and some of the role-play activities. You may wish to consult the office's behaviour logs and student OSRs before beginning this unit. Ensure that your school support team — including social workers, police liaison officers, or community support workers — knows you are addressing fighting in your class. You may wish to have one or more of these people speak to individuals or the class about fighting.

Fighting 101

Highlights

- Fighting is when someone acts aggressively towards other people. It can be a conscious attempt to hurt/intimidate, or it can be an uncontrolled, impulsive reaction.
- Some might turn to aggressive behaviour or fighting if they feel:
  - ☛ angry or annoyed
  - ☛ jealous or paranoid
  - ☛ scared or stressed out
  - ☛ confused or frustrated
  - ☛ blamed or criticized
  - ☛ put down or embarrassed
  - ☛ hurt or rejected
- Fights may start because of:
  - ☛ rivalry or playing dirty
  - ☛ bullying
  - ☛ feuds or taking revenge
  - ☛ misunderstanding
  - ☛ dissing someone, making a low blow, or blowing someone off
  - ☛ carrying weapons

Discussion Questions

- Can you think of a time when you felt really angry? Do you remember what caused these feelings? Are there certain situations that make you angry? What do you do when you get angry?
- Have you ever had someone get angry with you? How did it make you feel?
- Can you think of any situations where it might be okay to feel angry? Explain.
- Do you think fighting is wrong? Can you think of a situation in which fighting would be acceptable?
- How do you think fights get started? What could you do to avoid getting into a fight?
- Are there different types of disagreements? Do different people fight or argue differently? Why do you think so?
- How is fighting treated in the media? Are fights on TV or in the movies realistic? Why or why not?
- What does your school's Code of Conduct say about fighting? What are your school board's policies on fighting? How could you find out?

Teaching Activities

I = Individual   P = Pair   G = Group

Section	Subject Area	Activities
pp. 2–5	Media Literacy (I/G)	Ask students to watch one TV program and record the number of fights, the reason for each fight, and the effect of each fight on the different characters. Have students work in small groups to share and summarize what they discovered. Ask each group to elect one person to present their findings the class.
pp. 2–5	Language Arts/ Guidance and Career Education (G)	Make a three-column chart with the following headings: "Feelings," "Positive Choices," and "Negative Choices." Have students fill in the first column with the feelings listed on p. 4. Ask them to work in small groups to brainstorm different choices someone might make when they deal with these feelings. Have them fill in the rest of the chart and then discuss their ideas as a class.
pp. 2–5	The Arts (visual)/ Health and Physical Education (I)	Have students draw faces that express aggressive emotions. Encourage them to focus on how features, such as eyebrows, eyes, and mouths, help convey emotion. Students can work with a partner or use mirrors to note how to express different emotions.
pp. 6–7	Language Arts (I/G)	Photocopy the four comic strips. Cut them into frames and put the pieces of each comic strip into an envelope. Distribute the envelopes to students and ask them to put the pieces in order. When they are finished, ask them to draw or describe what might happen in the next frame. Have students present their comic strips to the class.
pp. 6–7	Language Arts/ Social Responsibility (I)	Have students choose a character from one of the comic strips. Ask them to describe what happened from their character's perspective, including their intentions, whose feelings were hurt by their actions, what they can do to make things better.
pp. 8–9	Mathematics/ Guidance and Career Education (G)	Divide the class in to six groups, and assign each group one of the ways to start a fight. Have students create a Venn diagram, labelling one circle "Instigator's Feelings" and the other "Defender's Feelings." Each group completes the diagram, ensuring that they include feelings that both parties share in the overlapping section. Have each group present their findings and discuss them as a class.
pp. 8–9	Mathematics (I)	Over a specific period of time, have students tally the number of times they witness each of the ways to start a fight at school, at home, or in the media. Have them graph their data and discuss their findings.
pp. 10–11	The Arts (drama) (G)	Using the quiz as a starting point, students work in small groups to create a skit about how to deal with fighting in a positive way. Have students present their skits to the class.
pp. 10–11	Language Arts (G)	Have students choose a question from the quiz. Use a Think-Pair-Share strategy to discuss various responses and to explain their answers to the question in greater detail.

The Instigator

Highlights
- The Instigator is the person who starts the fight by verbally or physically challenging another; by not trying to solve the problem; or by trying to make the problem bigger.
- The Instigator may start fights because he or she:
  - ☛ has been exposed to violence, neglected, or abused at home
  - ☛ has low self-esteem and is looking for acceptance or respect
  - ☛ needs to feel in control
  - ☛ needs to release feelings of anger, frustration, or revenge
  - ☛ feels peer pressure
- You can avoid being the Instigator by:
  - ☛ burning off your aggression with physical activity
  - ☛ doing something that helps you relax
  - ☛ taking a few minutes to calm down
  - ☛ talking to someone you trust
  - ☛ walking away from arguments or situations that make you feel aggressive

Discussion Questions
- Does it matter who starts a fight? Why or why not?
- Do you think that fighting is normal for boys? Is it normal for girls? Is there a difference in what is acceptable for boys and girls? Explain your thinking.
- Can another person make you angry? If so, who is in control of your emotions?
- What are "logical consequences"? Can you think of some examples?
- Does fighting always bring the same consequences? What might the different consequences be in instigating a fight with a principal, peer, or parent?
- What do you think might be some characteristics of an Instigator? Are there any other names we might use instead of Instigator (i.e., Bully)?
- Has there ever been a time when you were the Instigator? How did you feel in that situation?
- How do you think the other people involved might have felt? What were the results of this situation? How might you have handled things differently?
- Imagine that you are caught between two friends who are fighting each other. What might you do to help resolve the situation?

Fighting

Teaching Activities

I = Individual   P = Pair   G = Group

Section	Subject Area	Activities
pp. 12–13	Science (G)	Have students work in small groups to find out about fighting and aggression in animals (i.e., territory, dominance, etc.). Based on their findings, the groups create visual and oral presentations about the reasons why animals display aggressive behavior and how it is the same or different from people.
pp. 12–13	Language Arts/ Guidance and Career Education (I/G)	Ask students to match Dr. Shrink-Wrapped's eight reasons why people may turn to fighting with the sure-fire ways to start a fight on pp. 8–9. Ask students to explain why they think people might act out their feelings in these ways. Have volunteers present their ideas to the class.
pp. 12–13	Media Literacy/ Social Studies (I)	Have students collect news articles on instigators causing conflict in their community. Ask them to summarize the reports, noting the causes, actions, and reactions. Have them write a paragraph explaining what they might do to help resolve the problem.
pp. 14–15	Mathematics/ Social Studies (I/G)	Have students work through the quiz. When they are finished, ask them to work together to brainstorm three positive solutions to each situation described. Have students rework the quiz into a survey, using their solutions as choices a, b, and c. Ask them to survey students in other classes and record the results. Have students graph and discuss their findings.
pp. 14–15	The Arts (visual) (I)	Have students choose one of the ten situations from the quiz and create a "What To Do If…" poster. Their posters should outline the situation and what they can do to deal with it in a positive way. Display the posters around the classroom.
pp. 16–17	Language Arts/ The Arts (visual) (G)	Ask a volunteer to lie down on a large piece of bulletin paper and trace his or her outline. As a class, brainstorm what people think when they are in aggressive situations or fights and record the ideas in the head section. Then brainstorm a list of how people feel in these situations and record the ideas in the body section. Based on the other lists, come up with actions people might take to solve the problem and record them in the leg section. Display your finished poster in the classroom as a reference for future discussions.
pp. 16–17	Language Arts/ Guidance and Career Education (I)	Have students read through the six strategies given and choose which would best for them. Encourage them to write letters to themselves outlining the steps they will use to avoid getting into fights.

The Defender

Highlights
- The Defender is the person being harassed by the Instigator.
- The Defender may avoid fighting by:
    - ☛ avoiding arguments and staying away from bullies or people who get into fights
    - ☛ apologizing or talking to the Instigator to try to understand his or her point of view and find alternative solutions
    - ☛ letting people know when something is bothering you and how you would like to be treated
    - ☛ asking a teacher, counsellor, parent, or other trusted adult for help
    - ☛ finding strength in numbers to avoid being alone with the Instigator

Discussion Questions
- Is there a difference between a fight and a conflict? Explain your thinking.
- When is it important to stand up for yourself? What are some ways that you might defend yourself without getting into a fight?
- Do you think it possible to always avoid fighting? Is there ever a time why it might be okay to fight?
- How can you avoid becoming the target of an aggressive person?
- What are the characteristics of the Defender? Are there some negative names that people call the Defender? Do you think it is okay to call them these names? Why or why not?
- Would you defend yourself from a peer differently than you would from an adult? Why?
- Does there always have to be someone who is right and someone who is wrong? Does the Defender have to be right to win?

Teaching Activities

I = Individual   P = Pair   G = Group

Section	Subject Area	Activities
pp. 18–19	Social Responsibility/ Media Literacy (I/G)	Have students use the Internet to find out more about conflict resolution. Have students use their findings to create a "Top 10 Tips to Avoid Fighting" poster. Ask students to present their posters to the class.
pp. 18–19	The Arts (drama) (G)	Ask students to work in pairs to dramatize a conflict situation using one of the "Don'ts." Then have them repeat the drama using one of the "Do's." As a class, discuss how making positive choices turned each conflict into a win-win situation.
pp. 20–21	Mathematics (G)	Divide the class into groups of five and assign each group one of the tricks. Over the course of a week, have students tally the number of times they see other students utilize the trick. Encourage them to make notes about the incidents they observe, including whether or not the trick worked. Have students graph and draw conclusions from their results. Ask each group to present their findings. As a class, use the data to decide which trick works best and why.
pp. 20–21	Language Arts (I)	Have students write a story from a Defender's point of view. Encourage them to think about how their character might use one of the tricks to resolve the situation. Students may present their stories to the class or to a group of younger students.
pp. 20–21	The Arts (music) (I)	Have students use the tricks on pp. 20–21 or the "Do's and Don'ts" on p. 19 to write a poem or song lyrics about how to avoid fighting. Encourage them to share their songs or poems with younger students.
pp. 22–23	Language Arts (I/G)	Ask students to imagine they are a conflict counsellor or peer mediator. Have them choose one of the scenarios and write a dialogue demonstrating how each party feels and giving suggestions on how to create a positive solution. Students may wish to act out their dialogues for the class.
pp. 24–27	Language Arts (P)	Have students work in pairs to draw a web for one of the situations in the quiz. The situation should go in the centre, and there should be a branch for each option. Have students brainstorm for possible outcomes for each option and record them on their webs. Ask each pair to present their web to the class.
pp. 24–27	Language Arts (I)	Have students write a choose-your-own-adventure story based on one of the situations in the quiz. Ask them to think about what the consequences might be if the characters chose each of the options listed. Have them write brief stories for each of the options, describing what happens to the characters when they choose that response. Students can share their stories in small groups, or they can be compiled into a class book.

The Witness

Highlights
- The Witness is the person who sees a fight and has a responsibility to help ensure people don't get hurt.
- The Witness may be able to help by:
  - ☞ offering support to someone who is being picked on
  - ☞ seeking help when a fight breaks out
  - ☞ talking to someone if a fight has upset you
  - ☞ telling a responsible adult if someone is carrying a weapon
  - ☞ thinking about the alternatives to fighting

Discussion Questions
- Have you ever witnessed a fight? What did you do?
- When do you leave people alone to sort out their own problems? How do you tell when it is time to get involved?
- What is the difference between someone who tells and someone who is a tattle tale?
- Is there a difference between witnessing a friend get into a fight than when it is a stranger?
- Have you ever lied to protect a friend who has been fighting? How did you feel?
- Do you think more fights are caused by conflicts between two individuals or by conflicts among groups of people? Why?
- Do you think a Peer Mediation program would work at your school? Why or why not? Could we try it in our classroom?
- How can you be an honest witness and not get stuck in the middle of a conflict situation?

Teaching Activities

I = Individual   P = Pair   G = Group

Section	Subject Area	Activities
pp. 28–29	Language Arts/ Media Literacy (I)	Review acrostic poetry with students. Have them write an acrostic poem about a Witness' experience. You may wish to have students look for examples on the Internet to help them get started.
pp. 28–29	Language Arts (I/G)	Have students research to find out about local kids' help services, such as Kids' Help Phone and guidance counsellors. Ask them to create brochures that would encourage other students to use these services. Ensure that they highlight key services and contact information.
pp. 28–29	Language Arts/ The Arts (visual)/ Social Responsibility (G)	Have students work in small groups to create a Snakes and Ladders game based on the "Do's and Don'ts" section on pp. 17, 19, and 29. Use the "Do's" for the ladders and the "Don'ts" for Snakes. Ensure that students include instructions for their games. Have groups exchange games and follow the instructions. You may wish to have groups complete peer reviews of the games and give feedback on how they might improve the instructions. Encourage students to play their games with their families or share them with younger students.
pp. 30–31	The Arts (drama) (G)	Have students work in small groups. Ask them to choose one of the five scenarios and the solution that they think would be the best way to resolve the conflict. Have them role-play the situation and what might happen if the Witness followed their selected solution. Students may perform their plays for the class or a group of younger students.
pp. 30–31	The Arts (visual) (I)	Ask students to create a poster outlining the steps witnesses should follow to help resolve a conflict. Display the posters in the classroom.
pp. 30–31	Media Literacy (I)	Ask students to think about how they feel when they see a fight during a telecast of a sporting event, such as hockey or baseball. Have them write an opinion piece about whether or not they think that fighting should be allowed in sports. Ask them to provide examples to help support their arguments. Students may wish to read their reports to the class, or you may wish to have a classroom debate about the issue.

Gossip:
Deal with it before word gets around

People spread gossip everyday. It can be as simple as dishing the latest on celebrities or as hurtful as spreading a nasty rumour or someone else's personal secrets. Because gossip is so pervasive in our society, it is often difficult for adolescents to know how harmful it can be. *Gossip: Deal with it before word gets around* was created to help students tell the difference between sharing information and gossiping and to give them suggestions on how to deal with gossip before it gets out of hand.

In this resource guide to *Gossip*, teachers are given a range of discussion questions and activities to help students transfer the skills they learn in the classroom to their own lives. To get the most out of your class discussions and activities, it is important to create an open atmosphere and a positive classroom community where students feel comfortable sharing their experiences and opinions.

Before You Begin

Here are some tips and suggestions to help plan your Gossip unit:

- Gather as much material as you can about gossip, including *Gossip: Deal with it before word gets around* (see More Help on page 32 for a listing of materials).
- Decide on the scope of your study, depending on the grade level you teach and the needs of your students.
- Display books for children on this topic. In addition, prepare a bulletin board for posters, pictures and, as the theme develops, your students' work.
- Decide on the amount of time that you plan to spend on this theme.
- Have students brainstorm a list of emotions that they have felt because of gossiping and post the words on the bulletin or on a poster in the classroom. At the end of the unit, ask students to brainstorm a list of words that describe feelings that they have when they handle gossip well.
- Be aware that some of the subject matter covered in the book and resource guide may not be suitable for all students. Carefully review the content and be aware of any sensitivity before presenting it in your classroom.

Gossip 101

Highlights

- Gossip is talking or spreading rumours about someone else. It can range from talking about people because we care or are concerned about them, to sharing a good story, to digging up and spreading nasty information about them.
- Rumours and gossip can include:
  - ☞ speculation
  - ☞ secrets
  - ☞ slander
  - ☞ insinuation
- Gossip can be started by:
  - ☞ telling someone else's secret
  - ☞ making up a story or lying about someone
  - ☞ criticizing people behind their backs
  - ☞ sharing news that may not be true
  - ☞ starting or spreading a rumour
  - ☞ guessing something might happen and telling people it already has
- Gossip can happen to anybody anywhere: at school, in the workplace, and at home. It is important to think about what you say about other people to make sure that you are not causing harm with your words.

Discussion Questions

- How would you define gossip? What are some of the reasons why people might gossip? How is gossip different from talking to a mutual friend about someone you care about? Explain your thinking.
- Have you ever participated in gossip at your school? How did it make you feel? How do you think the target of the gossip would feel if he or she knew about it? Did this gossip have consequences for the people who were spreading it or the person they were gossiping about?
- What do you do when you hear gossip about someone? Do you tell the story to someone else or do you ignore what you heard? Does it depend on the people and the story involved? Explain your thinking?
- Do you think adults are affected by gossip as much or more than children? Why or why not?
- What role do the media play in encouraging gossip? Have you ever visited celebrity gossip Web sites or watched entertainment TV shows? Why do you think so many people are interested in the lives of celebrities?
- What might some of the negative effects of gossip be on the person being talked about? What negative effects might gossip have on the person spreading it?
- How could you let a Gossiper know you weren't interested in hearing the rumours without offending or hurting them? How else might you deal with gossip in a positive way?

Teaching Activities

I = Individual   P = Pair   G = Group

Section	Subject Area	Activities
pp. 2–5	Language Arts/ Guidance and Career Education (G)	Have students demonstrate how a story can be distorted as it is passed around by having them play a game. Tell one student a story and have him or her whisper it to another student. Continue this until the story has made its way through all the students. Ask the last person to hear the story to repeat it to the entire class and discuss how stories can become distorted as they are passed between people.
pp. 2–5	Media Literacy/ Social Studies (G)	Have students visit the PBS Kids website (http://pbskids.org/itsmylife/ quiz/rumors.html) and take the Raging Rumours quiz. As a class, discuss the reasons given for some of these rumours being so enduring: fear and the "yuck factor." Have students share their thoughts on why some urban legends stick around so long they are taken as fact and the influence of the Internet on spreading gossip.
pp. 6–7	Language Arts (G)	Write the headings "Speculation," "Secrets," "Slander," and "Insinuation" on four sheets of chart paper and post them around the room. Divide the class into groups and have each group write an example of gossip under each heading. Discuss the examples given as a class and brainstorm ways to deal with each example in a positive way.
pp. 8–9	The Arts (drama) (G)	Working in small groups, have students choose a question from the quiz and role-play a positive solution to the problem. When each group is finished, discuss the situation and solution as a class, asking for other ways they might bring the situation to a positive resolution.
pp. 8–9	Language Arts/ Media Literacy (I)	Create a class blog for students to share their thoughts and ideas about gossip. Encourage them to discuss topics they address in class as well as examples of gossip they see in the media. Remind students that this is a forum for them to use to help them deal with gossip in a positive way and not a place for them to spread their own gossip.
pp. 10–11	Language Arts/ Social Studies (I/G)	Divide the class into two groups to debate the statement: "Girls gossip, boys don't." Allow each group time to research and prepare their arguments. Conduct the debate (you may wish to invite another class to moderate and judge the debate). After the conclusion, discuss how students might combat this and the other myths given about gossiping.
pp. 12–13	Language Arts/ Guidance and Career Education (I)	Ask students to write a recipe for gossip. Encourage them to think about what gossip is and why people might gossip. Have them include a list of ingredients and instructions on how to make gossip really juicy. Ask them to include a description of what their recipe will yield, including the negative consequences. Gather the recipes into a class Gossip Cookbook and use it as a reference for examples of gossip's negative effects.

Gossip

The Gossiper

Highlights

- Gossipers are people who love to be the first to know all the gossip. When they hear something really juicy about someone, even if they're not sure it's true, they itch to tell someone else.
- The Gossiper might not think there is any harm in telling his or her friends the rumours going around.
- You can help stop the spread of gossip by:
  - avoiding people who gossip and letting them know you aren't interested in their rumours
  - thinking before you speak. Question who the information might harm, why this rumour is being spread, why you would want to pass this information on, if this gossip will hurt someone else, and would the person be hurt if they knew what was being said about them
  - putting a stop to rumours and harmful gossip by refusing to pass it on
  - respecting other people's privacy
  - not listening to gossip that is mean or harmful
  - standing up to gossip bullies by telling them you think it is wrong to use their words to try to hurt others

Discussion Questions

- Do you like to hear a good story about someone even if it is gossip? How does hearing or spreading gossip make you feel? Why do you think gossip gives you these feelings?
- Do know someone who passes on information even though he or she knows it may hurt someone? How might you encourage someone not to gossip without hurting their feelings?
- Have you ever heard gossip about one of your friends? How did it make you feel? How did you respond to it? Did you tell your friend? Why or why not?
- Imagine that you were spreading gossip and you were confronted about the rumour you were spreading? How would it make you feel? How would you feel about the person asking you to stop spreading gossip?
- Do you think it is all right to tell someone else's secret if you think it is good news? Why or why not? Can you think of a situation in which spreading good information about someone would get you or the other person into trouble?
- Imagine that one of the popular groups at school likes to gossip about people outside of their group. Do you think that this would be a good group to join? Would you join in on gossip to be popular? How might you deal with this group in a positive way?
- How can you tell if information you hear is gossip or not? What are the signs that someone is gossiping? How could you make sure you avoid gossiping about others?

Teaching Activities

I = Individual   P = Pair   G = Group

Section	Subject Area	Activities
pp. 14–15	Language Arts/ Guidance and Career Education (G)	Have students work in small groups to read and discuss the "Dear Dr. Shrink-Wrapped" letters and responses. Encourage them to discuss why their responses might be different than those given. Using this as a starting point, have students create a Top Ten Tips list of ways to deal with gossip in a positive way. Compile the lists into a class book or have students present their tips to younger students.
pp. 14–15	Language Arts/ Guidance and Career Education (G)	As a class, have students draft a pact to cut down on gossiping. Ask them to write out the goals of the pact and the steps they will take to help each other curb the amount of gossip they spread. Encourage all students to sign the pact and display it in the classroom. Check in with students periodically to see if they are following the pact and which of their behaviours they are finding most difficult to curb.
pp. 16–17	Language Arts/ The Arts (drama) (G)	Divide students into small groups and ask them to play charades using the situations found in the quiz. Have each group act out a different situation and ask the rest of the class to guess what they represent. After each group is finished, discuss the positive and negative affects that the situation might have on the people involved.
pp. 16–17	Language Arts (P/G)	Have students work with a partner to read through the quiz and determine which of the categories from p. 6 each statement falls under. Ask volunteers to present their ideas to the class and discuss as a group.
pp. 18–19	Media Literacy/ Social Studies (P)	Have students work in pairs to research news stories about Internet gossip and cyberbullying. Have them write a brief summary of one example and give suggestions on what the people involved might do to resolve the situation in a positive way. Ask volunteers to present their findings to the class.
pp. 18–19	Language Arts/ Media Literacy (G)	Ask students to work in small groups to find out more about a gossip or tabloid magazine, or an entertainment news TV show. Encourage them to find out their format and philosophy, what types of stories they feature, and the stories behind some interesting headlines. Based on their findings, have them create their own magazine or news show devoted to preventing gossip and rumours. Have students present their magazine or show to the class.
pp. 18–19	Language Arts (I)	Have students write a newspaper editorial on the effects of gossip. Encourage them to consider the negative affects gossip might have, how to stop the spread of gossip, and examples to support their argument. Compile the articles into a class paper.

The Subject

Highlights

- The Subject is the person who is being gossiped about.
- The Gossiper usually picks a victim who they know others will be interested in chatting about, such as:
  - popular kids
  - unpopular kids
  - smart kids
  - disadvantaged kids
  - kids who are different in any way
- If you find yourself the subject of gossip, you can:
  - investigate the cause to try to find the source and the reason for the gossip
  - stay cool and don't let the bully get to you
  - avoid resorting to revenge to solve the conflict
  - protect your privacy to make sure that your private information stays private
  - don't gossip about others
  - keep your good friends close and treat them with respect

Discussion Questions

- How would you feel if you were the Subject of gossip? What could you do to help protect yourself from gossip? How might you stop gossip once it has started?
- Why do you think someone might pick on people because they are different in some way? How do you think the Gossiper feels when they spread a juicy story about someone else? How do you think the Subject feels?
- Imagine that you heard a member of the popular group gossiping about your best friend. What might you say to the Gossiper? What would you say to your friend?
- What are some ways in which gossip is spread? How could you minimize your chances of becoming the Subject of gossip spread in these ways?
- How might technology be used to spread gossip? How could you use technology to tell people about the negative effects of gossip and encourage them to avoid gossiping?
- Who could you talk to if you were the Subject of gossip? How might they help you?

Teaching Activities

I = Individual   P = Pair   G = Group

Section	Subject Area	Activities
pp. 20–21	The Arts (visual) (G)	As a class, discuss the "Do's and Don'ts" section. Have students work in small groups to choose one Do and one Don't. Ask them to create a poster demonstrating how to use this Do and Don't to deal with being the Subject of gossip.
pp. 20–21	Language Arts/ Guidance and Career Education (I)	Have students write a journal entry about how they deal with gossip now and how they could deal with gossip in a more positive way. Ask them to include three steps that they will take to help them achieve their goal.
pp. 22–23	Language Arts (G)	As a class, review the letters to Dr. Shrink-Wrapped and discuss the responses. Have students write their own anonymous letter asking for advice on dealing with gossip. Collect the letters and redistribute them. Have students write a helpful response to the letter they receive. Gather all the letters and responses together in a class scrapbook.
pp. 22–23	Language Arts/ Media Literacy (G)	As a class, discuss the ways that technology can help spread gossip faster than word of mouth. Then, discuss ways that students can help protect themselves from gossip spread using technology. Have students create a brochure for younger students, warning them about the hazards of Internet gossip and cyberbullying and giving them tips on how they can protect themselves.
pp. 24–25	The Arts (drama) (G)	Have students work in small groups to role-play one of the ways they can deal with being the Subject of gossip. When each group has presented, ask students to suggest ways they can incorporate these tips into their own lives.
pp. 24–25	Language Arts/ Media Literacy (G)	Have students work in small groups to find a scene in a movie or TV shows that deals with gossip. Ask students to rewrite the scene so that the characters deal with gossip in a positive way following suggestions given in this book. Students can create a storyboard for their scene or act it out for the class.

Gossip

The Witness

Highlights
- The Witness is a person who hears gossip. He or she might not know if what they have heard is true or what to do with the information.
- When you witness gossip, you have can chose to:
  - ☛ spread the stories you have heard and propagate the gossip
  - ☛ tell your friends to stop gossiping until they know what really happened.
  - ☛ find out what really happened and get the facts straight
  - ☛ ignore the gossip and rumours

Discussion Questions
- Have you ever been around when someone told a story about another person? What did you do? How did it make you feel?
- Have you ever stood up to someone spreading gossip? What happened? How did you feel?
- Imagine that a new student comes to your school and people start gossiping about him and what happened at his old school. How do you think that might make the new student feel? What might you do to help stop the gossip? How do you think people might react to you?
- What are some ways that you could stop rumours that you hear?
- How do you feel when you hear rumours about someone you know? What could you do to help support the person being gossiped about?
- Does reading gossip magazines or websites make you a Witness? Why do you think people like to read gossip about celebrities? Do you think that these magazines or websites ever go too far? What might some of the consequences be for the celebrity involved or for the magazine or website?

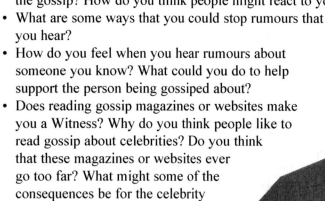

Teaching Activities

I = Individual   P = Pair   G = Group

Section	Subject Area	Activities
pp. 26–27	Language Arts/ Guidance and Career Education (G)	Have students draft an agreement with their friends and family members to deal with gossip in a positive way. Ask them to include tips on how to avoid gossiping. Encourage them to get as many friends and family members as they can to sign the pact to stop gossiping.
pp. 26–27	Language Arts/ Guidance and Career Education (G)	Have students work in groups of five to prepare a presentation about gossiping for a younger class. Encourage them to create games or skits that would appeal to younger students. Ask groups to perform their presentations for the class for feedback and then present them to a younger class.
pp. 28–31	Mathematics (G)	Using the quizzes in this book as a guide, have students create a survey to find out how their peers feel about and deal with gossip. Encourage them to think about what questions they can ask to find out how students deal with gossip and what kind of initiatives they think might work to help reduce gossip in your school. Have students conduct their surveys and record their results. Ask them to present their findings and discuss them as a class.
pp. 28–31	Language Arts/ Guidance and Career Education (I)	Have students write a persuasive letter to their principal encouraging him or her to help stop gossip in your school. Encourage students to include at least three reasons why they think the principal should try to reduce gossip and suggest one or two ideas on what could be done. Have students peer edit their classmates' letters and then submit them to the principal.
pp. 28–31	Guidance and Career Education (I/G)	Have students write three things that they want to make sure they do when they find themselves Witnesses to gossip. Encourage students to keep their lists handy and try to implement them. Revisit the lists occasionally throughout the year to see if students are implementing their changes, how they feel about gossip, and how people react to them when they avoid gossiping.

Racism:
Deal with it before it gets under your skin

Racism is a sensitive but important topic. Students in today's society must be aware of and sensitive to the traditions and beliefs of their classmates. They may sometimes find it difficult to recognize discriminatory or racist behaviour or know what to do when they encounter it. Few people would consider themselves racist, yet we might think about or treat people whom we see as being different than us in a negative way. *Racism: Deal with it before it gets under your skin* was created to encourage students to think about how they see and treat other people and how they can deal with racism in a positive way.

This guide to *Racism* aims to help create a supportive classroom where students will have the confidence to voice their concerns and participate in discussions that help them identify their values and beliefs and make conscious, responsible decisions.

Before You Begin

Here are some tips and suggestions to help plan your Racism unit.

- Gather as much material as you can about racism, including *Racism: Deal with it before it gets under your skin*. (See More Help on p. 32 of *Racism* for a listing of materials.)
- Decide on the scope of your study, depending on the grade level you teach and the needs of your students.
- Display books for children on this topic. In addition, prepare a bulletin board for posters, pictures, and, as the theme develops, your students' work.
- Decide on the amount of time that you plan to spend on this theme.
- Have students bring in their own books and movies that deal with racism to discuss. You may wish to make this a rotating display, asking different students to bring and present their selections on different days.
- Make a class K-W-L-S chart with the following headings: "What I Know," "What I Want to Know," "What I Learned," and "What I Still Want to Know." After you complete each section of *Racism*, fill in the chart as a class. Use this chart as a basis for discussion and a guide to which activities might be most useful to your students.
- Draft a template for a note of congratulations for kids that do a good job of dealing with racism throughout the year. When you notice a student doing well, write a personalized comment on the letter acknowledging that they've done a great job.
- Be aware that racism is a very sensitive subject that can touch different people in different ways. This book offers a variety of real-life situations that students may find themselves in, but all the topics discussed may not be appropriate for all students. Be sure to review all the content thoroughly to make sure that it is suitable for your students.

Racism 101

Highlights
- Racism begins with the idea that people can be divided into groups called races, which are based on physical traits.
- Racism is a form of prejudice. It is a belief that some races are superior to others and should have more power than others.
- Racism can come in the form of excluding, assuming, blaming, or labelling others based on their "race" or ethnic background.
- Racial stereotypes are usually negative and can lead to discrimination. Racism occurs when someone has the power to act on his or her racist attitudes.
- Racism can happen at school, in the workplace, and at home. It can happen to anybody.

Discussion Questions
- How would you define racism? Have you ever experienced racism in your school? How did it make you feel? How do you think the target of the racism felt?
- Have you ever heard racist jokes? How did it make you feel? How could this joke hurt someone's feelings? What might you say to someone who tells racist jokes to get them to stop but not offend them?
- Do you think adults are affected by racism more than children? Explain your thinking.
- Have you ever felt left out because of your ethnic background? How did you feel? What did you do about it?
- Do you think the media — television, the Internet, advertisements, music videos, etc. — plays a role in racism? Do you think the media uses racial stereotypes? Explain your thinking.
- Have you ever assumed something about a person just because of the way they look or act? Has anyone ever had anyone make assumptions about you based on the way you look or act? How did it make you feel?

Teaching Activities

I = Individual   P = Pair   G = Group

Section	Subject Area	Activities
pp. 2–5	Language Arts/ The Arts (visual) (G)	Have students work in small groups to create a poster to help stop racism. Encourage them to come up with a slogan and images that will get people to pay attention and think about their attitudes towards others. Have groups present their posters to the class and display them around the classroom.
pp. 2–5	Social Studies/ Media Literacy (I)	Have students collect ads for cars, clothing, or sports equipment from newspapers, magazines, and the Internet. Ask them to compare two different ads for similar products. Have them decide who the target audience is for each ad and how each one tries to reach that audience. Ask students to compare how different ethnic groups are portrayed in different ways. Ask students to present their findings to the class, using the two ads to demonstrate their findings.
pp. 6–7	Language Arts (G)	Write the headings "Blames," "Labels," "Excludes," and "Assumes" on four sheets of chart paper and post them around the room. Divide the class into groups and have each group write an example of racism under each heading. Discuss the examples given as a class and brainstorm ways to deal with each example in a positive way.
pp. 8–9	The Arts (visual)/ Language Arts (I)	Ask students to think about what it would be like to wear their attitudes towards racism. Have them design a T-shirt with a slogan to help stop racism. Encourage them to be creative. Have students present their designs to the class and display them around the classroom.
pp. 10–11	Language Arts/ Guidance and Career Education (I)	Have students anonymously write a "Dear Conflict Counsellor" letter about an issue involving racial prejudice. Compile the letters into a class message board, including blank pages on which students can write responses, and post it in the room. Ask students to respond to at least one letter, offering advice on how to deal with the situation in a positive way.
pp. 10–11	Language Arts/ Social Studies/ Media Literacy (G)	Have students watch the Historica Minute about Jackie Robinson (see www.histori.ca). As a class, discuss how Jackie must have faced prejudice from spectators, the opposing teams, and even his own teammates. Have students create a storyboard for a history minute about another incident in Canadian history involving racism, such as the internment of the Japanese during WWII or First Nations people being sent to residential school. Encourage them to focus on individuals and how they combated prejudice in their own lives. Have students present their storyboards to the class.
pp. 12–13	The Arts (visual) (I)	Have students create a collage of myths about racism. Encourage them to include images that display the emotions that they associate with prejudice. Ask volunteers to present their collages to the class and display them around the classroom.

The Minority

Highlights
- The Minority is the person who feels outnumbered and is treated differently by the Majority.
- Some people believe negative stereotypes about the Minority.
- You can respond to racism by:
  - ☛ acting powerlessly and allowing yourself to be negatively affected
  - ☛ becoming empowered and dealing with racism in a positive way
  - ☛ acting overpowered, or aggressively, which only promotes hate and intolerance
- You can help protect yourself from racism by:
  - ☛ exploring your feelings and trying to identify attitudes and behaviours that make you feel like an outsider
  - ☛ speaking up if you experience discrimination in any form
  - ☛ being proactive and joining clubs and groups that make you feel welcomed
  - ☛ exploring your history and being proud of your roots
  - ☛ educating yourself to find out more about the history of racism

Discussion Questions
- Who decides what groups of people are the Minority? Why do they get to decide?
- Do you ever feel like an outsider? What is it about other people's behaviours that make you feel this way? What are some things you could do to help yourself feel less like the Minority?
- Where do you think negative stereotypes about the Minority might come from? How do these stereotypes spread? Why do you think these stereotypes persist?
- Has someone ever made a racist comment to you? How did it make you feel? How did you respond? Can you think of a positive way to discourage someone from making racist comments about you or anybody else?
- If you are the Minority, how could you make yourself feel more empowered? How can you make sure that you don't act overpowered or aggressively towards the Majority?
- What are some ways that the Majority might make the Minority feel welcomed? Why is it important for both the Minority and the Majority to work together to fight racism?

Teaching Activities

I = Individual   P = Pair   G = Group

Section	Subject Area	Activities
pp. 14–15	The Arts (visual) (I)	Ask students to choose a "Do" and a "Don't" on p. 15. Have them use pictures and words to create a poster that contrasts the "Do" with the "Don't." Have students present their posters to the class and discuss why they chose the images they used.
pp. 14–15	Guidance and Career Education (I)	Have students research to find our more about ways that people can empower themselves to overcome racism. Ask them to create a brochure that demonstrates tips on becoming empowered.
pp. 16–17	Social Studies/ Canada and World Studies (P)	Have students work with a partner to complete the quiz. Ask them to choose one of the scenarios and research to find a real-life example of a similar situation (e.g., Sikh RCMP officers fighting for the right to wear turbans, Asmahan Mansour being prohibited from wearing her Hijab in a soccer tournament). Have partners present their findings to the class and discuss the issues. Encourage students to think about how the people involved might resolve the situation in a positive way that makes everyone feel empowered.
pp. 16–17	The Arts (drama) (G)	Have students work in small groups to act out a situation from the quiz, asking the other groups to guess which situation they are portraying. After each presentation, ask students to discuss how the people involved might have felt and how the situation would be resolved if they followed the empowered behaviour suggested.
pp. 18–19	Language Arts/ The Arts (visual) (G)	Divide the class into five groups and assign each group one of the ways you can protect yourself against racism. Have them design a bookmark displaying "tips" on what to do when they feel angry. Have students share their bookmarks with classmates.
pp. 18–19	Language Arts/ Social Studies/ Canada and World Stories (I)	Have students review the "Did You Know?" section and select one of the facts given. Ask them to research to find out more about the fact and then write a newspaper editorial expressing their opinion of the situation and suggesting ways to improve it. Have them share their editorials with their classmates and discuss their ideas.

The Majority

Highlights
- The Majority is the person who is an insider. He or she may believe and act on negative stereotypes about the Minority.
- People may be afraid or intolerant of differences because:
  - ☞ things we don't understand make us uncomfortable
  - ☞ we may have heard our parents or friends make unkind remarks about minorities
  - ☞ we see stereotypical images on television and the Internet
  - ☞ we are afraid of not fitting in
  - ☞ we might not be aware of the privileges and advantages we have
  - ☞ we don't realize that our attitudes and behaviours harm others
- You can help stop racism by:
  - ☞ examining your own behavior and attitudes toward people who are different from you and opening your heart and mind
  - ☞ learning about the history of racism to help expand your knowledge and understanding
  - ☞ questioning the images you see in the media and identifying the misinformation behind stereotypes
  - ☞ cleaning up racist graffiti in your community
  - ☞ telling people about and celebrating the International Day for the Elimination of Racial Discrimination (March 21)
  - ☞ speaking to your friends and helping them to change any negative behaviours
  - ☞ working to unlearn any prejudices you have

Discussion Questions
- What are some examples of racist behaviour? What would you do if you encountered any of these behaviours? How might you deal with them in a positive way?
- How is the Majority portrayed in the media? Why do you think the media uses stereotypical images of the Minority? Can you think of any examples of negative stereotypes that you see? How might being aware of these stereotypes in the media help you become empowered against racism?
- Are there any groups at your school or in your community that exclude minority groups? Are there any minority groups that exclude the Majority? How might we work to bring these two groups together?
- If racism is learned, how do people learn it? What influences people to become racist? How might they unlearn these attitudes and behaviours?
- What are some ways we can stop racism? How could we implement changes in our school or community to help stop racism?
- How would you define hate crimes? Why do you think these types of crimes are considered so serious? Explain your thinking.

Teaching Activities

I = Individual   P = Pair   G = Group

Section	Subject Area	Activities
pp. 20–21	Language Arts/ Social Responsibility (I)	Have students review the letters to "Dear Dr. Shrink-Wrapped." Encourage them to write their own questions about racism and to sign it with a pen name. Have them place their questions in a class mailbox. Students will then pick a question from the box and write a response to it. They may wish to research, interview, or share personal experiences to give their best response to the question selected. Post the letters and responses on a message board in the classroom and encourage students to add to it as they explore this topic further.
pp. 20–21	Social Studies/ Canada and World Studies (G)	Have students work in small groups to look at a story from different angles. Ask them to find a news story that made headlines across Canada or around the world. (You may wish to have them visit www.newseum.org or similar Web sites to find headlines.) Have them research to see how different news agencies covered the story. Ask each group to present their findings to the class and discuss how looking at the same story from a different perspective might help them deal with racism in a positive way.
pp. 22–23	Mathematics/ Guidance and Career Education (G)	Have students work in groups of three or four to develop a survey based on the questions in the quiz. Ask them to survey students in their school to find out their feelings on personal differences and racism. Have them analyze their data and display the results by grade level and gender. Ask them to share their findings with the class and discuss which data and responses surprised them. As a class, brainstorm ways you might work to change racist attitudes in your school or community.
pp. 24–25	Language Arts/ Media Literacy (G)	Have students work in groups of three or four to create a storyboard for a Public Service Announcement (PSA) to help stop racism. Encourage them to use the tips given on pp. 24–25 and to include details on the characters, dialogue, music, and sound effects they will use to help get their message across. Ask students to present their PSAs to the class, explaining their choices and how they think they will help other people stop racism.
pp. 24–25	Language Arts/ Media Literacy (I/G)	Ask students to make a slideshow demonstrating the "Do's and Don'ts" on p. 25. Encourage them to include images, graphics, music, and sound effects to help illustrate their slideshows. Have them present their slideshows to the class and discuss as a group how following these Do's and Don'ts can help stop racism.
pp. 24–25	Language Arts/ Canada and World Studies/ Social Studies (P)	Have students work in partners to create an information page about a person who has contributed to the fight against racism (e.g., Nelson Mandela, Rosa Parks, Elijah Harper). Ask them to research to find out about their person and to write a brief biography about them. Encourage them to include images and details that help give a sense of their person's work to fight racism. Compile the information pages into a Directory of Heroes that students can refer to throughout this lesson and the school year.

The Witness

Highlights
- The Witness is a person who sees prejudicial attitudes and behaviours.
- The Witness might think that racism is too big for one person to change.
- Witnesses may be afraid to speak up against racism because they think they might:
    - ☞ lose friends
    - ☞ interfere in something that is none of their business
    - ☞ be accused of being overly sensitive
    - ☞ get someone in trouble
- You can help be a positive force for changing racism by:
    - ☞ educating yourself about racism and other cultures
    - ☞ treating everyone with respect
    - ☞ getting help from a trusted teacher, parent, or older friend
    - ☞ setting a good example for others

Discussion Questions
- Have you ever spoken up when someone made a prejudicial comment? How did you feel? How did others around you react?
- Imagine that a good friend starts making racist comments to another friend just to become part of the popular crowd. What would you do? How could you explain to your friend that the behaviour was harmful without hurting his or her feelings?
- What are some ways that you could be a good example for others on how to stop racism? Give some examples of what you might do.
- Who could you turn to when you witness racism? How might they help you?
- Do you think that people can be somewhat racist? Is there a tolerable level of prejudice? Explain your thinking.

Teaching Activities

I = Individual   P = Pair   G = Group

Section.	Subject Area	Activities
pp. 26–27	Social Studies/ Physical Education (G)	Have students work in groups of five to play a game of "Four Corners" using the "Do's and Don'ts" on pp. 15, 21, and 27. Ask four students to stand in the corners of the squares and the fifth student to be It. Read the Do's and Don'ts in random order, leaving off the Do or the Don't at the beginning of the statement. If the students on the corners believe that the statement is a Do, they can try to switch places with someone on another corner, and the person who is It can try to take one of the corner places. If the statement is in fact a Don't, a student that tried to move then becomes It. When everyone has a chance to be It, bring the students together and discuss how the Do's and Don'ts might help them deal with racism in a positive way.
pp. 28–31	Language Arts/ The Arts (I)	Have students fold a sheet of paper in half. On one half, ask them to illustrate a situation from the quiz. On the other half, have them illustrate a solution that would bring a positive resolution to the situation. Ask students to present their illustrations to the class and discuss how their solution helps combat racism.
pp. 28–31	The Arts (drama) (G)	Have students work in groups of four to create a skit based on one of the situations in the quiz. Their skit should have two endings. The first ending shows the Witness choosing not to get involved in a situation and the consequences of that choice. The second ending should show the Witness taking steps to get involved and what the consequences of their actions are. Have students present their skits to the class and discuss the differences between the positive and negative outcomes.
pp. 28–31	Language Arts/ Canada and World Studies (G)	Have students work in small groups to find out more about the International Day for the Elimination of Racial Discrimination or other events that celebrate diversity (i.e., National Aboriginal Day, Folklorama in Winnipeg). Ask students to present their findings to the class. As a group, discuss how these celebrations help fight racism and make Canada stronger as a society. You may wish to plan your own class party to celebrate the cultures of your students.

Teasing:
Deal with it before the joke's on you

Teasing is a type of humour that points out someone's faults or idiosyncrasies. It can be used to show affection, but it can also cause harm by embarrassing someone or hurting their feelings. *Teasing: Deal with it before the joke's on you* and the accompanying resource guide were created to give students suggestions on how they can be more aware of the negative effects teasing can have and how to address conflicts that can arise when teasing goes too far.

It is important that students understand that while humour has its place, it is never all right to use humour as a weapon to hurt or bully others. As they explore the different situations given in the *Teasing* book and work with the suggested discussion questions and activities in this guide, they will learn the difference between good-natured ribbing between friends and when teasing goes too far. By exploring this topic from different perspectives — the Joker, the Picked-on, and the Witness — students will feel included and get a chance to see other sides of the issue. This approach will give students the opportunity to share their own experiences and learn from their fellow students.

Before You Begin
Here are some tips and suggestions to help plan your teasing unit:
- Gather as many materials as you can about teasing, including *Teasing: Deal with it before the joke's on you*. (See More Help on page 32 of *Teasing* for a listing of materials.)
- Decide on the scope of your study, based on the grade level you teach and the needs of your students.
- Prepare a bulletin board for posters, pictures, and, as the theme develops, your students' work.
- Encourage students to bring in their own books and movies that deal with teasing. Ask volunteers to present their materials as part of the discussions.
- Draft a template for a note of congratulations for kids that do a good job of dealing with teasing throughout the year. When you notice a student doing well, write a personalized comment on the letter acknowledging that they've done a great job.
- Decide on the amount of time that you plan to spend on this theme.

Teasing 101

Highlights
- Teasing is a common way to share humour with the people around you by:
  - playing keep-away
  - sharing practical jokes
  - tickling
  - mimicking someone
  - tantalizing someone with a secret
  - tempting someone with a treat
  - keeping someone guessing
- Teasing can be a way of showing affection for another person, but it can also be used to embarrass people and hurt their feelings. When teasing is meant to hurt someone, it is a form of bullying.
- People may tease each other to exclude, make a point, embarrass, or intimidate.
- Some people might tease because they have learned that:
  - people like to be entertained
  - people notice them when they tease others
  - they feel powerful when others seem afraid of them
  - they like to be the center of attention
  - they can get away with it
  - they think it is acceptable to pick on other people
- Teasing can happen to anyone, anywhere.

Discussion Questions
- How would you define teasing? Do you think this is an acceptable form of humour? Why or why not?
- Have you ever teased anyone in an affectionate way? How is this different from teasing someone in order to hurt him or her? Explain your thinking.
- Have you ever been teased? How did it make you feel? How did you feel about the person teasing you?
- Have you ever thought up different nicknames for people? Has anyone given you a nickname? What was it based on? Do you think this is teasing? Are there some nicknames that are unacceptable? Explain your thinking.
- When does teasing become hurtful? What are some examples of hurtful teasing?
- Do you think adults tease each other? Can you think of any examples of adults teasing each other in the media? Do you think adults can be hurt by teasing?
- How might you tell if someone is just joking with you or if they are really making fun of you? How might you talk to them about the teasing and let you know you don't appreciate the jokes?

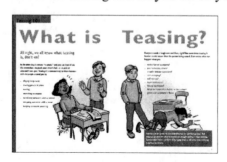

Teaching Activities

I = Individual   P = Pair   G = Group

Section	Subject Area	Activities
pp. 2–5	Language Arts/ Mathematics (I/G)	Tell students that they are going to be "Teasing Detectives." Over a period of two to three days, have them record all the teasing that they notice, noting where and when they see it, who was doing it, and what it was about. Have students tally and graph their results. Ask students to present their findings to the class and discuss them as a group.
pp. 2–5	The Arts (drama) (G)	Divide the class into small groups. Ask each group to come up with a situation to role-play based on the lists on pp. 4–5. Have each group present their play to the class and ask the other groups to decide if the situations are funny (someone is just joking) or if it is hurtful teasing. As a class, discuss what they can do to resolve the situation in a positive way.
pp. 6–7	Language Arts/ Guidance and Career Education (P/G)	As a group, brainstorm a list of words that might be associated with teasing and record them on the board. Have students work in pairs to discuss why they associate these words with teasing, what emotions they connect to these words, and situations in which these feelings might come up. Ask pairs to present their findings to the class and discuss how this activity helped them to think about teasing in new ways.
pp. 8–9	Social Studies/ Media Literacy (G)	Have students work in small groups to research news stories about current events that involve teasing (e.g., cyberbullying, politicians poking fun at each other, etc.). Encourage students to think about how teasing is treated in the media. Have students present their findings to the class and discuss the place of teasing in the media and what it has taught them about teasing in the classroom.
pp. 10–11	Language Arts (I)	Have students write an anonymous "Dear Conflict Counsellor" letter asking for advice on a problem involving teasing. Ask them to exchange and answer someone else's letter, offering them advice and support.
pp. 12–13	Language Arts/ Media Literacy (G)	As a class, design a web page to help prevent teasing. Have students work together to decide on the content and how it will be laid out. Encourage them to write articles and helpful tips. Ask them to look for other websites that they can link to for further information. As a culminating task, have students create the pages of their website by hand or using design software.
pp. 12–13	Guidance and Career Education (G)	Have students form a teasing support group for the school. Ask them to think about the goals of the groups and what services they would. Have students create a poster or brochure to promote their group.

The Joker

Highlights

- The Joker is the person who likes to laugh and to make other people laugh. Jokers enjoy entertaining people, but they need to be aware that their jokes might hurt other people's feelings.
- You can try to stop hurting others with your teasing by:
  - ☛ learning the difference between gentle teasing and bullying
  - ☛ considering other people's feelings
  - ☛ listening to how other people joke and trying to learn how to be funny without being cruel
  - ☛ trying to be sensitive how people around you respond to your jokes by watching their expressing
  - ☛ trying to make people laugh without teasing them

Discussion Questions

- Have you ever teased anyone? How did they react? Did they look embarrassed or unhappy when you teased them? How did their reactions make you feel?
- How do you think you would feel if someone said hurtful things to you but claimed to just be teasing? Would you consider it harmless teasing or bullying?
- How might people around you react if you said something funny about someone else? Do you think they would all share your sense of humour? What would you do if they told you that they did not like your teasing? Would you stop or would you think they had no sense of humour?

- Imagine that you love to pull practical jokes all the time. What would you do if your friends started to avoid you because of this? Would you try to find out what bothered them or would you find new friends?
- Imagine the new kid in your class decided to tease people before they have a chance to pick on him. How might you let the new kid know that this is not a good way to make a first impression? How might you get him involved with your friends so he did not feel the need to tease others?
- Who could you go to if someone is teasing you too much? What might they do to help?
- How do you react when you see someone always teasing another person? How do you think the Joker might feel? What are some reasons why the Joker might single someone out and tease him or her?

Teaching Activities

I = Individual   P = Pair   G = Group

Section	Subject Area	Activities
pp. 14–15	Media Literacy (I/G)	Ask students to find examples of commercials that show the characters teasing each other. Have volunteers present or describe the commercials to the class. Encourage them to think and talk about the target audience and how the characters are using teasing to market the product (i.e., Who is being teased and why?) Ask students to give their opinions on whether or not these commercials are effective and how the advertisers might have achieved the same results without using teasing.
pp. 14–15	The Arts (drama) (G)	Have students work in small groups to role-play situations that involve teasing. Encourage them to explore the feelings of everyone involved and how they might resolve the situation in a positive way. Have them present their plays to the class and ask the other groups for suggestions on other ways the situation might have been handled to achieve a positive outcome.
pp. 16–17	Language Art (P/G)	Have students work in pairs to complete the quiz. When they are finished, ask them to write a poem or rap to encourage other students not to tease, encouraging them to be creative and use humour to help get their message across. Have volunteers present their poems or raps to the class.
pp. 16–17	Guidance and Career Education (G)	Have students work in small groups to create a 20-minute lesson about teasing for a class of younger students. Ask them to include the issues they want to discuss, how they will approach these issues, and activities to help younger students understand these issues. Have the groups present their lessons to the rest of the class or to a class of younger students.
pp. 18–19	Language Arts (I)	Draw students' attention to the first two bullets in the "Did You Know?" section. Ask them to find a similar example of teasing in the media and research to find out more about it. Encourage them to think about why advertisers and comedians tease and how audiences respond. Have them prepare a report on their findings and present it to the class.
pp. 18–19	Language Arts/ Physical Education (G)	Have students work in small groups to mime situations that demonstrate how to use the tips on how to stop hurting others with teasing. Encourage them to use their body language and facial expressions to convey emotions. Have groups present their mimes to the class and discuss them as a class.

The Picked-on

Highlights
- The Picked-on is the person who is teased. Although the Picked-on may want to fit and have a good sense of humour, he or she may also feel bullied and humiliated.
- There are three ways to respond to being picked-on repeatedly:
  - ☛ In Your Face — getting back at the teasers
  - ☛ Hide your Face — taking the teasing and hiding your hurt
  - ☛ Face Up — standing up to the person teasing you and letting him or her know that she isn't funny
- When you are tired about being teased, you can try:
  - ☛ keeping your cool and ignoring the teasing
  - ☛ being prepared with a good come back
  - ☛ gently challenging the teaser and letting him or her know that you have had enough
  - ☛ showing determination and telling the teaser that if he or she doesn't back off you will ask your parents or a teacher to step in
  - ☛ asking a teacher or parent for help if none of your other approaches work

Discussion Questions
- Have you ever been teased or picked-on? How did it make you feel? How did you react?
- What are some ways that you might stop someone picking-on or teasing you without offending him or her and making it worse? How do you think he or she might react?
- Do you think that teasing is a legitimate form of humour? Why or why not? Is there anything that should be off limits to teasing? Explain your thinking.
- What happens when someone tells a politically incorrect joke? How does it make you feel? Should you say or do anything when someone tells an inappropriate joke? Why or why not?
- What might you do if you tell someone to stop teasing you and he or she doesn't listen? Who might you turn to for help? How might you resolve the situation in a positive way?
- Would you hold a grudge against someone who teases you, even if they apologize? What might you do to feel better and learn to let go of the hurt they caused?
- How might you keep your cool when someone starts to pick-on or tease you? What could you do to help control your anger and frustration? Who could you talk to about your feelings?
- How might you protect yourself from being teased at school or at home? What are some ways that you could deal with teasing in a positive way?

Teaching Activities

I = Individual   P = Pair   G = Group

Section	Subject Area	Activities
pp. 20–21	Physical Education/ Guidance and Career Education (G)	Have students play a game of Elbow Tag. Each student locks elbows with a partner. Then one student is picked to be The Picked-on. In order to be "safe," the Picked-on must lock arms with someone. To do so, he or she must suggest a positive way of dealing with teasing (based on the "Do's and Don'ts" on p. 21). When he or she locks arms with someone, the other partner then becomes the Picked-on and must find a new partner to link arms with. Continue play until all students have had a chance to be the Picked-on. When the game is finished, discuss how students might apply the "Do's and Don'ts" in real-life situations.
pp. 20–21	Language Arts/ Media Literacy (I)	Have students use the "Do's and Don'ts" on p. 21 as a starting point to create a slideshow that illustrates the emotions the Picked-on feels. Encourage them to use images, graphics, words, and music to help enhance their slideshows. Have students present their slideshows to the class, asking their peers to explain what emotions they feel while watching and comparing them to what the creator had in mind.
pp. 22–23	Social Studies/ Mathematics (G)	Have students work in small groups to create a survey to find out how students in their school deal with teasing. Encourage them to use the quiz as a starting point and think about the type of questions they will ask in their survey to get the data they need. Have them conduct their surveys and display the results. Ask them to discuss their findings as a class and decide if there is a correlation between teasing and age or gender. Have them write up their findings as a class and display them in the classroom.
pp. 22–23	The Arts (visual) (G)	Have students work together to create a mural showing positive outcomes to the situations in the quiz. Ask them to include speech/ thought bubbles and captions to show what the characters are feeling and how they handle the situations effectively.
pp. 24–25	Language Arts/ Media Literacy (G)	As a class, brainstorm a list of good (gentle) comebacks the Picked-on could use when he or she is teased. Divide the class into three groups and have each group write a dialogue for a short film or podcast that demonstrates how the Picked-on might use a gentle comeback to dissuade the Joker from teasing. Have each group present their dialogue to the class and discuss how successful the comebacks were.
pp. 24–25	Social Studies/ Guidance and Career Education (G)	Have students read the information about political correctness on p. 25. Divide the class into two groups and have them debate the statement: "No one should ever make jokes that offend anyone, anywhere, at any time." Allow groups to research and prepare their arguments, encouraging them to find examples to support their opinions. Conduct the debate. (You may wish to have another class moderate and decide on a winner.) Afterwards, discuss what students discovered about humour and political correctness and whether or not their opinions changed.

Teasing

The Witness

Highlights

- The Witness is a person who sees someone else getting hurt or causing hurt by teasing.
- If you don't speak up when you see others doing wrong, it suggests you're going along with it. By not standing up for your beliefs, you are part of the problem.
- Humour can be a difficult thing to share, understand, or even explain. A good rule of thumb to follow is that if a joke embarrasses or hurts anyone, then it is not okay.
- If you are the Witness, you can help by:
    - ☞ asking the teaser to listen if someone asks him or her to stop teasing
    - ☞ supporting someone who has been teased
    - ☞ reporting hurtful remarks to teachers or parents

Discussion Questions

- Have you ever been around when someone took teasing too far? How did it make you feel? How do you think the person being teased felt? If you found yourself in the same situation, what might you do to help?
- Have you ever stood up to someone teasing another person? If not, what stopped you from saying something? How do you think you would feel if you spoke up against teasing? If you have spoken up, what happened? How did the people involved react? How did you feel?
- How could you tell if teasing has gotten out of hand? What might you do to resolve the situation without upsetting the people involved?
- Imagine witnessing a bully teasing his victim. You would like to do something but you are afraid that he may start picking on you. What could you do to help in this situation? Explain your thinking.
- Imagine that one of your friends always makes jokes at other people's expense. He says these jokes don't hurt anyone as long as they don't hear him. How could you tell your friend that this type of humour isn't appropriate without offending him? What might you do to make sure that no one gets hurt?
- How might you help someone who is being teased? What could you do to make him or her feel better?
- What feelings do you associate with teasing? Do you think that all people feel this way? If teasing could hurt the Teaser, why not use it against him or her?

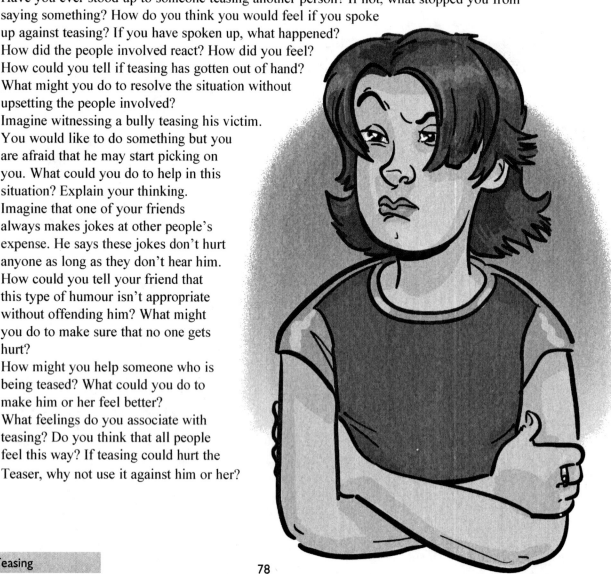

Teaching Activities

I = Individual   P = Pair   G = Group

Section	Subject Area	Activities
pp. 26–27	Language Arts (G)	Have students work in small groups to find stories that involve teasing and note how the characters handle the situations. Have them write a new ending for the story in which the characters deal with teasing in a more positive way. Ask them to share their endings and discuss them with the class.
pp. 26–27	Language Arts (G)	Have students create a graffiti wall on which they express their feelings about being a Witness to teasing and the "Do's and Don'ts" on p. 27. Display the graffiti wall in the hallway, leaving space for others to add to the wall. Discuss the comments that people add with the class.
pp. 26–27	Language Arts/ Guidance and Career Education (I)	Have students write a journal entry about how they deal with teasing. Encourage them to think of a time when they were teased or they were a Witness to teasing. Have them to describe the situation and what they did. Then, ask them to write two suggestions on how they might have handled the situation in a more positive way and how the outcome might have been different. Based on this, have them write a list of three tips they should follow the next time they are involved in teasing. Ask students to review their tips periodically to see if they are able to implement them.
pp. 28–31	Guidance and Career Education (G)	Hold a class meeting in which students come up with ten classroom rules for dealing with teasing. Have them create a poster of their rules and display it prominently in the classroom.
pp. 28–31	Language Arts/ Guidance and Career Education (G)	Write the following sayings on the board: • Sticks and stones may break my bones, but names will never hurt me. • Teasing is just a natural part of growing up. • Jokes are just fun — they don't hurt anybody. Divide the class into three groups and assign one saying to each group. Ask the groups to decide if they agree or disagree with these statements and to write down at least three reasons to support their decision. Have each group present their reasons and discuss them as a class.
pp. 28–31	The Arts (drama) (G)	Have students role-play different situations found in this section, including ways of reaching a positive solution. Discuss the plays and solutions as a class.

Teasing

Contributors

Wendy Doucette has been a teacher-librarian for the past fifteen years and is presently a Resource/Reading Recovery teacher. She lives with her husband and three children in Greenvale, PEI.

Rachelle Duffus has been teaching in the greater Toronto area for over ten years. She has been a specialist in Reading and Special Education for both Behaviour and Learning Disabilities. Rachelle has designed several win-win programs including the inter-generational Adopt-A-Grandparent and MYIND: Mentoring Youth in New Directions, a program for at-risk students. She is currently an Itinerant Behaviour teacher for the Toronto District School Board.

Yolanda Hogeveen, B.Ed., M.L.S., is a high-school teacher-librarian. She develops and teaches Library Technician courses for Red River Community College in Winnipeg, MB, and is the co-author of teachers' guides for the videos Pioneer Quest and Quest for the Bay.

Heather Jessop is a teacher-librarian with the Peel District School Board in Ontario. She has previously co-written curriculum documents for her school board and the Elementary Teacher's Federation of Ontario.

Harriet Zaidman is a teacher-librarian in Winnipeg, MB. She reviews children's and young-adult books for CM: Canadian Review of Materials as well as adult books for The Winnipeg Free Press.

Additional Resources

Arguing
- http://www.4children.org/chdev.htm#ang: The Action Alliance for Children site contains articles on teaching anger management and conflict resolution.
- www.education-world.com: The Education World website provides strategies for dealing with anger management issues in the classroom.
- www.emints.org/ethemes/resources/S00001717.shtml: The eMINTS website includes teaching tips and activities promoting conflict resolution skills.
- www.PollDaddy.com: PollDaddy.com provides a free tool to create surveys and polls.
- www.SurveyMonkey.com: SurveyMonkey.com allows you to quickly and easily create surveys.

Bullying
- www.bullyingcanada.ca: BullyingCanada.ca is an anti-bullying website dedicated to Canadian youth.
- www.cca-kids.ca: Concerned Children's Advertisers' website offers a variety of Public Service Announcements about bullying prevention.
- www.cdli.ca/CITE/bullying.htm: The Centre for Distance Learning & Innovation website provides resources for teachers and students on bullying.
- www.kidshelpphone.ca: Kids Help Phone provides an online resource for kids and teens on bullying and cyberbullying.
- www.safecanada.ca: The Government of Canada's Safe Canada website includes links to information regarding public safety and bullying in Canada.
- Beane, Allan L. *The Bully-Free Classroom: Over 100 Tips and Strategies for Teachers K–8.* Minneapolis, MN: Free Spirit Publishing, 1999.
- Rigby, Ken. *Stop the Bullying: A Handbook for Teachers.* Markham, ON: Pembroke Publishers Ltd, 2001.
- Sanders, Pete. *What Do You Know About Bullying?* Markham, ON: Fitzhenry & Whiteside Limited, 2004.
- *The Big Deal About Bullying.* DVD. McIntyre Media Inc., 2005.
- *Bullying: You Don't Have to Take It Anymore.* DVD. Human Relations Media.
- *Teen Truth: An Inside Look at Bullying and School Violence.* DVD. Human Relations Media.

Cyberbullying
- www.cybersmart.org: Cybersmart provides online workshops for safety and security online and cyberbullying.
- www.bewebaware.ca: Be Web Aware is a website run by the Media Awareness Network with information on how to report online problems and how to involve your community to help kids stay safe online.
- internet101.ca: Internet 101 was created by a committee of police forces and RCMP.
- Cyberbully411.com: This site is aimed at preventing cyberbullying.
- SurveyMonkey.com: Survey Monkey is a tool to create an publish custom surveys.
- *Adina's Deck.* Adinasdeck.com. 2007.
- *Sarah's Story.* Internet101.ca: http://internet101.ca/en/cyberbullying.php
- *Let's Fight it Together.* Childnet: http://www.digizen.org/cyberbullying/fullFilm.aspx
- *Odd Girl Out.* Jaffe/Baunstein Films, 2005.
- Bryant, Annie. *Just Kidding: Beacon Street Girls #10.* New York: Simon & Schuster Books for Young Readers, 2009.
- McCaffrey, Kate. *Destroying Avalon.* Fremantle, WA, Australia: Fremantle Arts Centre Press, 2006.
- Hinduja, Sameer and Patchin, Justin W. *Bullying beyond the schoolyard: preventing and responding to cyberbullying.* Scarborough, ON: Nelson Education Ltd., 2008.

Cliques

- http://kidshealth.org/kid/feeling/friend/clique.html: How Cliques make Kids Feel Left Out
- http://kidshealth.org/teen/your_mind/problems/cliques.html: Coping with Cliques
- http://www.massgeneral.org/children/adolescenthealth/articles/aa_cliques.asp

Fighting

- http://actagainstviolence.apa.org: Adults & Children Together Against Violence educates communities and creates safe environments for children and youth.
- www.apa.org/releases/media_violence.html: This media release from the American Psychological Association provides information on childhood exposure to media violence.
- www.goodcharacter.com: This online teacher guide provides discussion questions and activities for character development and a variety of life skills.
- www.kidshealth.org: The Kids Health website provides answers and advice for teens about fighting.
- www.leaveoutviolence.com: Leave Out Violence's website is devoted to youth whose lives have been touched by violence.
- Drew, Naomi. *The Kids' Guide to Working Out Conflicts: How to Keep Cool, Stay Safe, and Get Along.* Minneapolis, MN: Free Spirit Publishing, 2004.
- Goliger, Janet. *I Need to Be Safe: I'm Worth It!* Sherman Oaks, CA: CLASS Publications, 2006.
- Schrumpf, Fred, Donna K. Crawford, and Richard J. Bodine. *Peer Mediation: Conflict Resolution in Schools.* Champaign, IL: Research Press Publishers, 1997.

Gossip

- www.bullyboy.ca: The Misadventures of Bully Boy & Gossip Girl website offers sections for teachers and kids.
- http://pbskids.org/itsmylife/quiz/rumors.html: The PBS Kids website includes a gossip quiz.

Racism

- www.pch.gc.ca/march-21-mars/: The Canadian Heritage website showcases information on the International Day for the Elimination of Racial Discrimination.
- www.unacorg/yfar: Youth Forums Against Racism is an initiative of the United Nations Association in Canada, launched in recognition of the United Nations International Year for the Elimination of Racial Discrimination.
- www.tolerance.org: Teaching Tolerance is dedicated to reducing prejudice, improving inter-group relations and supporting equitable school experiences, it is an Anti-racism Educational site.
- *For Angela.* DVD. National Film Board of Canada, 1993.
- *Playing Fair.* DVD. National Film Board of Canada, 1992.
- *Taking Charge.* DVD. National Film Board of Canada, 1996.

Teasing

- www.cca-kids.ca: Concerned Children's Advertisers' website offers a variety of Public Service Announcements about teasing and bullying prevention.
- www.howstuffworks.com: Visit this site and view the "Teasing: Playful Teasing and Hurtful Comments" and "Helpful Tips Teasing: Understanding the Effects of Teasing" videos.
- Blanco, Jodee. *Please Stop Laughing at Me: One Woman's Inspirational Story.* Avon, MA: Adams Media Corporation, 2003.
- Cooper, Scott. *Stick and Stones: Seven Ways Your Child Can Deal with Teasing, Conflict, and Other Hard Times.* New York, NY: Three Rivers Press, 2000.
- *Hurting with Words.* DVD. Human Relations Media, 1997.